TAROT: TALISMAN OR TABOO?

TAROT:

TALISMAN OR TABOO?

Reading the World as Symbol

Mark Patrick Hederman

CURRACH
PRESS

First published in 2003 by
CURRACH PRESS
55A Spruce Avenue, Stillorgan Industrial Park, Blackrock, Co Dublin

www.currach.ie

Cover by Anú Design
Origination by Currach Press
Printed in Ireland by Betaprint, Dublin

ISBN 1-85607-902-3

Acknowledgements

The author and publisher gratefully acknowledge the permission of the following to use material in their copyright: FRANCE CARTES GRIMAUD, B. P. 49 - 54132 Saint Max Cedex (FRANCE) for the images from l'Ancien Tarot de Marseille; The Pierpont Morgan Library/Art Resource, NY for s0068146 ART110922: Bembo, Bonifacio (fl.1447-1478) and Antonio Cicognara (15th CE). Wheel of Fortune (no.9). Italian tarot cards, made for the Visconti-Sforza family. MS. 630, f.9-10. © The Pierpont Morgan Library/Art Resource, New York, USA; Risteárd Mulcahy and Lorcan Walshe for Lorcan Walshe's painting 'The Tower'; *The Irish Times* and Seamus Heaney for 'Horace and the Thunder'; Faber and Faber for quotations from 'The Wasteland' by T. S. Eliot; Darton, Longman & Todd for the quotation from *The Jerusalem Bible*.

Every effort has been made to trace copyright holders. If we have inadvertently used copyright material without permission we apologise and will put it right in future editions.

To the Living Enneagram

The holy nine of the ninefold plan:

Tara's banqueting hall with nine places

Without any one of whom I would not be who I am

'Nine bean-rows will I have there, a hive for the honey bee'

And recognise the night in all nine of its faces

and to you,

unknown reader,

who may at times be touched

by the Holy Spirit

while reading this book,

as I was touched at times

while writing it.

Contents

PART I

CHAPTER ONE

WHY THE TAROT?

We live our lives in a tiny area of light, as if we were huddled under a sub-standard streetlamp. This small circle of visibility that surrounds us is what we call conscious life. We live and move in our day-to-day world within this orbit. But there is a vast area of darkness and of mystery beyond this floodlit patch. This outer darkness is what we call the unconscious.

The unconscious is that area of ourselves that is beyond the reach of our ordinary ability to reason, outside the realm of our day-to-day activity. It is a distinct area. As such it is vast, strange, hidden. We would hardly know it was there if we did not get inklings of it, whispers, rumours. That is why we have to use images from our familiar world to describe it.

Western culture has been constructed as a citadel within this vast labyrinthine forest. We have built ourselves impregnable walls and surrounded our compound with such fortresses and ramparts that for several centuries we were able to persuade ourselves that there was no reality, hostile or otherwise, beyond the frontiers of our self-constructed spaceship. Beyond consciousness and whatever was approachable by our reason there was nothing that need concern us. The ship became our universe, in almost complete denial of the ocean in which it was floating.

How this came about and how the mirage was maintained are interesting stories in themselves. What we have come to call Western culture at its most fundamental involved, and still involves, what can almost be described as an hypnosis. It has become commonplace to describe the rise of Adolf Hitler and the imposition of Nazi ideology on Germany, for at least one decade during the last century, as hypnotism of a whole people by processes ranging from propaganda to education. This somewhat chilling and clear-cut example can serve as a model for a less obvious, far more extended and much more global hypnosis that has spanned our Western world for at least three centuries. However, its roots go back very much further than the seventeenth century.

The ideals on which we Westerners base the conduct of our lives are hybrid and ancient, coming as they do from European philosophy at its earliest and most idiosyncratic. Most of our thinking was done for us by the Greeks. Their legacy was so solid and convincing that few thinkers coming after them gave their explanation a second thought. Why reinvent the wheel? If someone has done such a good job explaining the universe, why bother to revisit the archives? Western European philosophy since the Greeks has been described as a series of footnotes to Plato. But listen to the warning which has crept into our language and has taken on the wisdom of a proverb: *Timeo Danaos et dona ferentes*, I fear the Greeks especially when they come bearing gifts.

The phrase comes from Virgil's *Aeneid*, book II, and it will be worth our while to pause and examine it. The book describes the war between the Greeks and the Trojans. Its purpose is to show that Rome was a direct descendant of the Trojans. The book from which the above quotation is taken describes the way in which the Greeks tricked their enemies and overcame them. It tells also, although the author may not have been aware of this, how the Greeks eventually destroyed Rome as well. And stretching down the centuries it can also describe how the Greeks have had the power to destroy, in some way, each one of us.

The Trojan horse had been left behind by the Greeks, supposedly as an offering to Neptune for a safe return home. It was a massive wooden sculpture erected on the beach. The Trojans were meant to believe they had won the war and that their enemies had retired defeated. We too are meant to believe that the Greeks went home long ago as far as we are concerned, and that there is nothing left behind them on our beaches that we need worry about. Laocoon, Trojan priest of the sea-gods, warns his compatriots that this is a trick: 'Either some Greeks are shut inside this timber work, or it is a machine for overlooking our walls, perhaps to pry somehow into our homes and threaten us from above, or it contains some other kind of treachery; put not your trust in horses, my fellow countrymen, whatever it turns out to be, I fear the Greeks even when they are bearing gifts [or, perhaps, 'especially when they are bringing gifts].¹ With these words he heaves his spear into the rounded side of the horse's belly as if to prove its hollowness. Later, as Laocoon offers a bull in sacrifice to Neptune on the seashore, two sea monsters crawl from the ocean onto the beach, devour his two sons and then wrap themselves twice around his neck and his stomach and drag him after them behind the statue of Minerva, where we don't see exactly what happens to him. But he doesn't reappear.

The Trojans tremble at his fate and interpret it as punishment for Laocoon's sacrilegious attack on a gift to the Gods. They carry the horse into their city with ceremony and celebration. At midnight, from their hiding-place in the belly of the horse, the Greeks give access to their fellow countrymen, whose ships have only been hiding behind the island of Tenedos, a few miles from the land. A whole civilisation is thus destroyed. The question I ask is similar to that posed by W.B. Yeats: 'Is there another Troy for them to burn?' Have not all of us been somewhat burnt by the Greeks?

The destruction of Troy came from the sea, the depths of that underworld where monsters lurk. Minerva was Goddess of the dawn (her name connects with the Latin *mens* and the English 'mind'). The priest of the ocean deep and the prophet who warned against the Greeks was sacrificed on the altar of reason, the place of worship of the mind. Laocoon was sacrificed to the Goddess of mind, the dawning of consciousness. His neck and stomach were divided from his head.

What we inherited from the Greeks was a way of life, an explanation of ourselves, an architecture for civilisation. Most of our words to describe any of our important enterprises are Greek: politics, ethics, economy, philosophy, etc. The list is almost half of our vocabulary. Every time we invent or are overwhelmed by something new, we reach for a Greek word to label it. The 'tele', the 'phone', 'gamma' rays, 'micro'soft, 'paedophile', 'psychopath' are Greek words.

We may quite understandably think that we have changed considerably in the twenty or so centuries which separate us from the ancient Greeks, but they set the parameters and the direction so definitively, many centuries before the Christian era, that they determined both the limits and the quality of even our most recent lifestyles. Alexander Pope puts it in a nutshell:

'Tis education forms the common mind:
Just as the twig is bent, the tree's inclined.[2]

And let no one misquote me or get me wrong. I have nothing but the greatest admiration for the Greeks. What they contributed to all future development in the West is both ungainsayable and inestimable, from pharmacology to the Olympic Games, for instance. My point is that the corollary of such massive endowment was an impoverishment and debilitation in certain important and, since that time, neglected areas of our humanity.

Plato and the Greeks in general had a very pessimistic view of the human situation: human life is not much to boast about (*Republic*, 486 A); all flesh is trash (*Symposium*, 211 E); and the Laws describe mortals as sheep, slaves, puppets or toys of the Gods. Plato was not just a puritan, he was what Iris Murdoch[3] describes as 'a moral aristocrat'; he not only regarded most of the rest of us as irretrievable in terms of 'goodness', but he saw salvation as a kind of thinking. Philosophy, as a spiritual discipline, would allow people to change their lives and become 'good'. As F.M. Cornford[4] points out, the confidence that the Greeks placed in reason was based on the enormous strides being made by geometry at the time of Socrates. Geometry, as the name spells out, means measurement of our world. In Plato's view, reason was equal to the world, able to take its measure. *The Republic* seems to be based upon the assumption that there can be a world where everything is harmonious, where things can run like clockwork, where we, as human beings, can reasonably attempt to know ourselves and our world. The model for such a state of affairs is the clarified world of mathematics.

The legacy of Greek philosophy has been the belief that consciousness is our way to human perfection, and that the unconscious is an area to be avoided, sealed off, obliterated. Science as the adequate, efficient, omnivorous combined-harvester is required patiently to reap the universe and translate its harvest into mathematical formulae. The unconscious is relegated to the world of exterior darkness.

It was not just the unconscious that was ostracised. Anything irrational was also off limits. This meant that many aspects of what it means to be human were discounted as substandard, unworthy of the glorious title of 'rational animal'. And these pariahs are mostly connected with our bodies. Plotinus, who, after Plato and Aristotle, was perhaps the greatest formator of our Western world, was, we are told explicitly, ashamed of being in the body. He held, to quote him directly, that: 'Corporeal things ... belong to the kind directly opposed to the soul and present to it what is directly opposed to its essential existence'.[5] All this long before Christianity emerged to strengthen and universalise such prejudices.

Quite naturally Greek words became the vehicle for Christianity in many of its fundamental formulations. The unwritten teachings of Jesus Christ became articulated in systems of thought which were available and apparently compatible. These are essentially Greek patterns of thought, although fed also by other sophisticated local cultures. Neoplatonism, for instance, which was derived from the views of Plotinus, influenced a large part of early Christian doctrine and spirituality, especially through the writings of the so-called Pseudo-Dionysius, a sixth-century Syrian monk who was thought to be the New Testament convert of St Paul (Acts 17:34) and who deliberately forged his writings to pass as such, a deception that wasn't discovered until much later. His merging of Neoplatonic philosophy with Christian theology received almost apostolic status because he was believed to have been a contemporary of St Paul. And although it did provide some very beautiful and fruitful guidance towards a particular school of mystical experience, it also loaded the dice very emphatically against the body, corporality and physical self-expression. The result was and is a very admirable and very beautiful explanation of the universe and of ourselves. However, it is dangerous and detrimental because it makes serious errors of judgement about who we are, about what is essential to our nature and what is not, and, above all, what an all-powerful and all-perfect God would or would not find acceptable about our humanity. Our invitation to become 'children of God', which is what the Incarnation was about, when translated into this local culture, can be interpreted as an invitation to renounce being human and to set about becoming divine, to stop being animals and start being angels. The invitation is read as asking us to become the opposite of what we are as human beings. If 'spiritual' is interpreted in this way, it means renouncing or repudiating everything that is not spiritual, which means our nature, our flesh and, above all, our sexuality. In the *Philebus* (65–6), for instance, Plato seems to suggest that the very absurdity of sex is repugnant.

A distorted simplification of the complexity of humanity, an arbitrary selection of certain elements for cultivation and certain others for cauterisation, and the imposed authority of one particular faculty over all the rest:

these provided the groundwork for the socio-cultural and psychological labyrinth which became our Western heritage. An exaggerated emphasis on the 'spiritual' and a vilification of the 'physical' led to a glorification of the conscious and a repudiation of the unconscious. Reason rules and the irrational is outlawed.

One of the most obvious purveyors of the irrational is the imagination, and this is why the Greeks were ultimately suspicious of it. Art was out. In *The Republic* (398 A) any poets or dramatists who might visit the ideal state should be expatriated. Plato, like all dictators and most puritans, detested theatre. We can only imagine what he would have thought of television! He was aware of the danger of politically destructive ridicule and its subversive undermining of social stability. 'An old quarrel between philosophy and poetry' is broached in *The Republic* (607 B). Books III and X give an extended account. Aeschylus and Homer are dangerous subversives misleading the people by portraying the Gods as undignified and immoral and as subject to helpless and foolish laughter. Poets and playwrights should teach us to respect religion, admire good behaviour and learn that crime never pays. Unfortunately the theatre, in Plato's view, had become the hotbed of anarchy, the cauldron of vulgarity, the cynical caricature of civilised life. Aristophanes, for instance, makes a laughing stock out of Socrates through slanderous buffoonery, which vindicates the lowest aspirations and mediocre lifestyle of the great unwashed.

The irony, however, is that even while the Greeks were banishing art, the way they were doing so was itself art. Their moratoria would not have survived if they had not been conveyed through art works. Even Plato's *Dialogues* are works of art. Virgil is, of course, a consummate Latin artist, and the Trojan horse can be a metaphor for the way in which art got sneaked into the equation by the Greeks themselves, in spite of themselves. Ulysses, like Jacob, robbed them of their own birthright. The double-pronged tradition of rationalism and idealism at the top and myths, legends, poetry and theatre underneath, provided the schizophrenic structure which carried the germ of European civilisation. The wooden horse was itself a work of art. Inside, it was a blueprint for conquest, a war machine. But outside, it was a massive wooden sculpture. So, even the division between conscious and unconscious may have been a legacy of the Greeks, mathematics and geometry feeding the mind while myths and legends, like dreams, stock up the imagination.

Of course in the museum of history, art is voluminous and abundant, while philosophy is a skinny and unimpressive pamphlet in comparison! If there are two original philosophers in a generation, it is a major harvest. Most of these are men and, as Iris Murdoch has again pointed out: 'Moral philosophers, attempting to analyse human frailty, have produced some pretty unrealistic schemata' (EM 457). 'The explanation of our fallibility is more informatively carried out by poets, playwrights and novelists. It has taken philosophy a long time to enlist the aid of literature as a mode of explanation' (EM 457). Art accepts as a given the ambiguity of the human person. Indeed, great artists often seem to 'use' their own vices for creative purposes, so that 'the bad side of human nature is secretly, precariously, at work in art'. Where philosophy and theology are purists, art is a shameless collaborator, and Plato rightly identifies irony and laughter as prime methods of collaboration (EM 449). Laughter (as distinct from amused smiles) is undignified, explosive, something violent and extreme, offending against the modest sobriety that is, with such an impressive backing of theory, commended in the *Philebus*. Plato seems to equate an absurdity-rejecting dignity with some sort of virtuous self-respect. Thus the holy among us are recognisable by the length and straightness of their faces.

Now, for others, Christianity is a religion not of self-conquest but of self-surrender. Perfection is not as important as completion. Humility is the founding attitude that makes any further Christian virtue possible. Iris Murdoch puts it succinctly: '[I]t is worth asking the question whether one can be humble with unimpaired dignity' (EM 450).

If the twentieth century has taught us anything, it is that not only is it unhealthy to neglect the unconscious part of ourselves, but it may even be 'sinful,' if we understand this word as 'missing the mark'[6], or effectively ignoring the call to be human. The result of remaining unconscious, of not dealing with who we are, is that we become a danger to ourselves and to others, which is fine if we have no responsibilities. However, if we are called to be leaders or teachers, if we are in positions which affect the lives of other people, then the danger of not getting in touch with our unconscious is that, whether we mean it or not, even with the best intentions in the world, we end up doing evil.

Most of us are aware by now that the twentieth century was for many people a hell on earth and that this hell was a human creation. It was a hell of cruelty and mayhem resulting from the incapacity of powerful people to decipher their unconscious motivation, whether in concentration camps, institutions, schools, or families.

After the holocaust there should be no possibility of neglecting the unconscious in ourselves. We have to find out about our darkness, about the shadow side of ourselves. Whatever way we do it, whether through science or dreams or art, each of us has to discover and explore the labyrinth of the dark, the unconscious, the shadow side. The unconscious is slippery as an eel. We see glimpses but we cannot describe a shape. Its language is incomprehensible, even inaudible to most. But, no matter how difficult it is to decipher, such work must be undertaken. We must recognize that most of our past, whether personal or historical, took place underground, in silent rivers, ancient springs, blind pools, dark sewers. While the task of making these accessible to our consciousness is difficult, it is nonetheless imperative. Even more so at the beginning of a new century when we hope to outline some plausible tracks into a better future. We have to read the signs of the times, especially those that whisper to us from the depths of the earth. Early detection of volcanoes, for instance, can save lives. And the truth of what we are now, and of what we might be in the future, is mostly hidden underground.

It is also true that everything that happens in our world is indicative of who we are and how we are living on the planet. Significant events, however arbitrary and random they may seem, are coded messages about the behavioural patterns that preceded them. I don't mean this in any kind of moralising way, as though, for instance, natural disasters might be punishment for unseemly conduct. I mean that whatever we do and however we behave, our lifestyle and our attitudes towards the place where we dwell are bound to have effect upon the nature around us, whether that involves our own bodies or our total environment. The task of rendering such signs legible and accessible was in the past left to artists and so-called prophets. However, at this time we must learn to read such signs for ourselves. We can no longer abdicate or delegate this responsibility. Each one of us has to learn to decipher what is happening to us now, in a way that helps us to detect those silent underground symptoms that indicate the inappropriateness of our present postures, and the alternatives, which might hasten our assumption of a more authentic humanity.

The twentieth century was a blundering between ideologies. Ideologies are false futures drawn in big pictures by those who take it upon themselves to shape our destiny. These are inventions of some human mind rather than humble acceptance of what we really are. History as we have known it is mostly a concatenation of disasters, resulting from such attempts to impose a strait-jacket. The truth requires that we inch our way forward with constant reference to the subtler music of who and what we are. The future can be skewed. Mission statements, ten-year plans, vision documents, can be a way of imposing our own myopic architecture, of obliterating the splendour of what might have been: the future perfect.

There are a number of ways to gain access to the dark of our unconscious. The first is by being attentive to our dreams. We dream every night but we may not be conscious of it. It takes time and attention to let ourselves become aware of these dreams. They are the language of our unconscious telling us what we refuse to tell ourselves during our daylight hours. Nor are they easy to interpret. We have to learn to crack the code. We have to find out about our darkness, about the shadow side of ourselves. This is not a luxury, an optional extra. It is mandatory. Whatever is not made conscious is likely to be repeated. One of the major obstacles to dealing with this reality in an effective way is the refusal to admit that it exists at all, or the conviction that it is unnecessary to find out about it and integrate it into our psychological, our social, our educated selves.

Apart from our own dreamtime, there is also the great reminder of this reality contained in the stories of our ancestors. What dreams are to individuals, myths and legends are to peoples. Such a storehouse exists for all of us as peoples of the Western world, and these coded keys to our unconscious are mostly Greek in origin, or at least the version of it that has reached us was fashioned in that other, older aspect of Greek culture, their myths and legends.

Apart from the language of dreams and the storehouse of mythology, there is the phenomenon of art.7 However, many people feel uncomfortable with any of these three privileged modes of access. You hear it so often: Art means nothing to me. I can't even begin to understand it. And: I never dream, and even if I do, I can't remember any of it after I wake up.

However, in this battle-scarred and war-weary twenty-first century planet, we have begun to crack the code of such dreamlike indications. We have understood that gods and goddesses placed by antiquity in the heavens above or in the depths of the ocean below are to be discovered inside ourselves, deep in our own intestinal labyrinths. A valid question might be why we had to wait through twenty centuries before we woke up to this reality? Some say we couldn't face it until now, that we were unprepared for such exploration until the conscious side of ourselves had developed the tools that would be necessary both to achieve the exploration and to survive it. The development of these tools was made possible by concentrating our energies in the direction of conscious thought and not being distracted by less calculable concerns. In other words, it was only because we refused to acknowledge the existence of the unconscious that we were able to concentrate on making scientific consciousness the powerful weapon that it has become today. Science, as well as providing methods and equipment, also developed attitudes of mind: there was nothing we could not know, nowhere we could not explore. And now this has come full circle, with the conscious mind turning its attention to the unconscious.

Towards the end of the nineteenth century and the first half of the twentieth century, resistance to entry and discovery of the unconscious was particularly trenchant and totalitarian. Most fundamentalist movements in society were versions of religious thought systems, all of which waged war against art, for instance, as a kind of idolatry, whose purposes were presumed to be hedonist if not evil. The discovery of the unconscious by scientists and doctors was condemned as immoral, and all attempts to understand the reality of humanity as a bodily phenomenon were resisted as degradation of our true nobility as spiritual creatures of God.

One significant symptom of such a mind-set is the attitude to that most primal and expressive form of art which is dancing. After three years in Africa I am aware of how irretrievably impoverished most of us Westerners have become in this essentially human way of being. Dance is the manifestation of the spirituality of matter, demonstrating the most elegant and spiritual poise of our nature in its bodily aspect. It is both the accomplishment and the expression of well-being and the most fundamental and artistic way of attuning ourselves to the rhythm of the universe. It has been part of religious self-expression in most cultures the world over. It is the most natural way to participate in the liturgy, for instance. But in our religious education there is an endemic prejudice against it. Africans who have been trained in our religious ceremonies have in a few years not only lost their natural aptitude for it but have learned to despise it as an irreligious activity. The Bible itself is aware of such attitudes:

> David brought the ark of God up from Obed-edom's house to the Citadel of David with great rejoicing... And David danced whirling round before the Lord with all his might, wearing a linen loincloth round him. Thus David and all the House of Israel brought up the ark of the Lord with acclaim and the sound of the horn. Now as the ark entered the Citadel of David, Michal the daughter of Saul was watching from the window and saw King David leaping and dancing before Yahweh; and she despised him in her heart.
>
> As David was coming back to bless his household Michal, the daughter of Saul, went out to meet him. 'What a fine reputation the king of Israel has won himself today,' she said 'displaying himself under the eyes of his servant-maids, as any buffoon might display himself.' David answered Michal, 'I was dancing for Yahweh, not for them, and as the Lord lives ... I shall dance before him and demean myself even more. In your eyes I may be base, but by the maids you speak of I shall be held in honour.' And to the day of her death Michal, the daughter of Saul, was barren.
>
> (2 Samuel 6: 12–17, 20–23)

The attitude of Michal summarises our patrimony in Western European culture. It is part of the Greek and Roman inheritance. Most of the Fathers of the Latin Church, for instance, were opposed to dancing, having learnt their prejudices from the Greeks. Several saw it as 'evil' and linked to pagan worship. However, most contemporary educated 'pagans' were of a similar view. Sallust, Plutarch, Lucian and

Cicero condemn it explicitly, although the last mentioned is recorded as having varicose veins and swollen legs so, according to Renaissance writers, may have been condemning what was impossible for himself.

Ambrose of Milan (340–97) in his commentary on St Luke's Gospel (6, 8) says 'there is no compatibility between the mysteries revealed by the resurrection and the shameful contortions accomplished in the dance'. His convert Augustine (354–430), commenting on the psalms (XCI, 2), warns against desecrating Sunday with pagan practices. It would be better, in his view, to spend the Lord's day digging, despite the moratorium on work, than dancing. John Chrysostom (347–407), the golden-mouthed preacher of Christianity, in one of his homilies on St Matthew's Gospel (XLVIII, 3), says: 'Where there is dancing, there is the devil. It was not for this that God gave us feet that we might jump around like camels.' 'Everything should be full of chasteness, of gravity, of orderliness', he tells us in his Homily XII, 4, on St Paul's Epistle to the Collosians, 'but when I look around me I see the opposite: people frisking like mules and camels... And you might say if neither virgins nor married couples are permitted to dance, who will be left to accomplish this activity? My answer would be, no one – for what need is there of dancing?'

Such an example of how wrong we can be about one fundamental aspect of our lives shows us the possibility that we have been getting it all wrong at other more universal and all-embracing levels, listening too carefully to wrongheaded prescriptions about ourselves and our way of life. Many such prejudices have been splashed into the gene pool by our most intelligent ancestors. Let us, I say, take from the Greeks the extraordinary richness of their heritage but let us be fearful also lest they teach us to despise what is essentially our own. This is one of the important roles of the artist: to show us the beauty, the truth and the idiosyncratic pertinence of what is essentially ours. Science teaches us about human nature; art reveals to us the uniqueness of what it can mean to be human. I fear the

Greeks, especially when they are bearing such gifts as rejection of the body, disregard for the unconscious, disdain for art, disapproval of dancing. *Au contraire*, 'Zorba', I say with that great twentieth-century Greek artist, Kazanzakis, 'teach us to dance!'

The tarot cards, as well as teaching us to dance mentally, also provide us with an easier route to the unconscious. This alternative route uses some of the materials, shapes, signs and symbols used by artists and our dreams. Playing with the cards in a certain way helps us to cover the same area, using similar symbols and shapes, but in a more accessible and less daunting way. The tarot cards introduce us to a new kind of space and another kind of time. The space involved requires from us a kind of lateral vision; the time involved is experienced as coincidence, more professionally labelled synchronicity, another Greek word. The major arcana of the tarot are visual aids to the unconscious. They are vivid shorthand portraits, something akin to the Chinese ideograph or picture writing. These latter do not try to represent a sound, as other alphabets or musical annotations do; they abbreviate a person or a thing. The ideogram for 'sun' or for 'tree' in the more primitive Chinese alphabets is an outline sketch of these two realities; so much so that certain artists claim to be able to see these references immediately without having learnt the language. In a similar way, the pictures on the tarot cards are recognisable to all of us; they can be used as a visual slide-rule on which we can play out our own particular psychological equations.

Like the stained glass windows in Chartres, the tarot cards bring us back to a time before what we call the modern way of thinking started. They provide a window to an alternative world, another way of thinking. They are relics of a religious sensibility. Like secret agents in disguise they have been hidden as entertainment and as fortune tellers' gimmicks, but as such they are camouflage for a secret army.

Between the mystery and the structures we have

received as Church, Scripture, Tradition, there is an abiding testimony to the time before these were set in place. Such testimony was, of necessity, oral or visual, pre-literal stimuli. The tarot trump cards are 22 spiritual exercises through which we can immerse ourselves in the spirit of that living tradition. This requires an activity different from and deeper than academic study or intellectual explanation. Deep and intimate layers of the soul become active and bear fruit when we meditate on the arcana of the tarot. The cards are something like a ferment or an enzyme (Greek: *en* = in, *zeume* = yeast) which can stimulate the spiritual and psychic life. What they reveal are not secrets (things hidden deliberately by some human will) but *arcana*, which means what is necessary to know in order to be fruitful in the domain of spiritual life. In Latin, *arca* is the word for a chest; *arcere* the verb means to close or to shut. In English the word 'arcane' comes from this root. It means something secret or mysterious. The word is also used in such well-known artefacts as Noah's ark and the ark of the Covenant in the Hebrew Bible.

So, we can visit the 22 cards as if they were an art gallery. These trump cards also act as projection holders, hooks to catch the imagination. They represent symbolically those instinctual forces operating autonomously in the depths of the human psyche which Jung called the archetypes. It is from this unconscious part of ourselves that our relationship with the spiritual and the divine emanates, as does every other aspect of our relational being. The cards can be useful to us in either our vertical or our horizontal relationships. They can help to negotiate our passage through the world of the spirit as well as the world of other people.

Projection is an unconscious, autonomous process whereby we see in persons, objects and happenings in our environment those tendencies, characteristics, potentials, and shortcomings that really belong to ourselves. Every child is born with these hereditary projectiles; there is nothing we can do about it. But we can become aware of what we are doing at all times, and we can sketch out for ourselves the wardrobe or the cast that we are continuously projecting.

These major arcana of the tarot present us with a billboard of this star-studded cast. Hollywood has used them shamelessly and relentlessly: Charlie Chaplin, The Marx Brothers, Woody Allen, Audrey Hepburn, Grace Kelly, Ingrid Bergman, Charlton Heston, John Wayne, Ralph Richardson, Elizabeth Taylor, Joan Collins, Judi Dench, to name but a few from the the last century. All these are paid to be our archetypes of the silver screen. The tarot cards are a more basic and less romantic quiver of projectiles.

Although the specific form of these images may vary from culture to culture and from person to person, their essential character is universal. People of all ages and cultures have dreamed, narrated and sung about the archetypal mother, father, lover, hero, magician, fool, devil, etc. Religion has its own set of archetypal models: Francis of Assisi, Catherine of Siena, Elizabeth of Hungary, Louis VIII of France, Blanche of Castille, Gregory the Great, Margaret of Scotland, etc.

I hope to introduce you to this easy and available medium in the course of this book and show you why the tarot cards are a most valuable source of spiritual growth. The tarot pack is a way to meditate. It is a beautiful and attainable work of art. Anyone can buy a pack. You can carry it with you on a train, spread it out in your own room. For three centuries it has been hijacked by occultists and necromancers, to the extent that it has got a bad name. People flee from it. I have heard it called 'the devil's pack'. It has become something of a scapegoat. And yet, before this happened it was used in a perfectly harmless context and developed within the tradition of Christian symbolism. It can be for many people who find art inaccessible an alternative way of thinking artistically. And it could be for most, what I have seen described in other contexts as, 'an idiot's guide' to the unconscious.

There are other such methods and tools, some of them equally elegant and engaging. I think of the I-Ching, for instance. But this is essentially Asian in origin and character and therefore more difficult to access for Europeans. I prefer the tarot for myself because it is Western in its imagery. This is not for racist or chauvinist reasons; it is simply a realisation that there seem to be pools of the unconscious that underpin various landmasses or ethnicities. Dreams and myths testify to the regional clustering of such varied undercarriages. It does seem to be true that we share with others a common unconscious which connects with our genes, our culture and our stories. Nordic as opposed to Celtic mythologies, for instance. But at a more generic level, it is true that the Western world as a whole is penetrated by a particular unconscious and that this has been the origin of the strange figures that make up the 22 major arcana of the tarot pack.

Whatever way these cards have been used in the past or are being used in the present, I am proposing them here as unique manifestations of a deep, almost inaccessible part of ourselves which it is essential for us to access if we are to come to terms with the world we have created for ourselves to live in. These cards are a moving (in both senses of the word) kaleidoscope, a symbolic map of the penultimate layer of humanity. The only other access to this landscape we have, apart from our dreams, over which we have little control, is through the mediumship of artists. We generally misinterpret or fail to see what these mediums are saying to us until about a hundred years after they have spoken. Art is, after all, mining the unconscious in ways productive of its own forms. Only a small minority are gifted with this capacity. And yet each one of us is required to exercise such muscles to render ourselves capable of recognising these signs, these shapes, these symbols, these archetypes, these colours, if we are to find our way in the landscape which is emerging as the twenty-first century. Also it is the business of each of us and all of us to piece together the jigsaw of our collective unconscious. The tarot cards provide us with some interesting fragments, which we can pore over as an archaeologist might piece together fragments of some very ancient broken statue, to provide clues about the workings of some very ancient civilisation. That statue and that 'civilisation' are deep inside ourselves.

The cards can act as visitors from inner space. As psychological constructs, these 22 characters, the court cards of Europe, are archetypal figures emerging over the centuries from the depths of our unconscious. They are the way we meet the people of the world around us, the faces we project onto the faces that confront us every day of our lives.

The cards divide into recognisable groups: seven are women on their own; five are men; two show an angel with three human figures; two represent a pair of male figures; one is a bisexual devil with two prisoners: one male, one female; death is an indeterminate skeleton with a scythe who has just mown a field of human limbs, including two heads: one male, one female; the Wheel of Fortune shows three strange creatures made up of various animal parts; the moon is a sad-looking human face with two dogs baying in front of a pond containing a crayfish.

In other words, almost in the way that fairy tales or nursery rhymes carry an unconscious dictionary of human experience, these cards are a catalogue of our unconscious telephone directory. These are the pictures we use to paint the world of the people we meet. These are the archetypal features we project onto the different people who enter our world. Every woman we meet is potentially a divine vision or a spiritual guide; every man is either a dictator or a guru. And we resent them all for being such, even though it is we ourselves who have thus designated them.

However, that is reading the cards at a psychological or even sociological level. There is another spiritual way of reading them, which is the most fundamental aspect of this book.

CHAPTER TWO

TAROT IN THE PAST AND IN THE FUTURE

The origin of the tarot cards is shrouded in mystery and speculation. Fortunately, living as we do in the twenty-first century, we have the advantage of reliable historical scholarship, which can dismiss most of the far-fetched theories that have besmirched the image of these cards and prevented many if not most people from using them.

From the beginning of its recorded history this pack of cards was used to play a game, which still exists and is played today. The game is similar to the card game Bridge and would have been as popular in the sixteenth century, although not as widespread and universally available. The cards divided into four suits, as in the ordinary pack of cards today, except that an extra knight was added to our King, Queen and Jack, or Knave, bringing the total number of cards to 56, that is, four more than the average pack of 52 cards today. Added to these were 21 trump cards, plus a card called 'the Fool', which would have been equivalent to 'the Joker' in our contemporary pack. The name tarot is derived from these extra so-called 'trump' cards — it is a French adaptation of the Italian word *tarocco* (plural: *tarocchi*), previously referred to as *cartes de trionfi*. Triumph cards (Latin = *triumphi*), became 'trump' cards, which derives from the same word. From the first records we have, these 22 trump cards were standardised in both subject and order. They bring the total number of Tarot cards to 78.

The game was played similarly to our game of Bridge. You followed the suit that was initially played (suits were swords, clubs, cups, or coins, rather than spades, clubs, hearts and diamonds). If you had no card in this suit you were permitted to play a trump card. Points were awarded for each trick won.

The oldest pack of tarot cards in existence comes from Italy and dates from the fifteenth century. There are several versions. In 1975 the most complete of these was reproduced and made available. The originals can be seen in the Pierpont Morgan Library in New York.[1] These cards were bought by Pierpont Morgan from Count Alessandro Colleoni of Bergamo in 1911. The rest of the cards remain with the Academia Carrara and Colleoni family in Italy. The set was handpainted on heavy cardboard, supposedly by the Cremonese artist Bonifacio Bembo (circa 1420–1480). Experts have identified that either he or his workshop were responsible for at least some of these cards. Some would claim that six of this set, Fortitude, Temperance, the Star, the Moon, the Sun and the World, must be later fifteenth-century replacements, for technical reasons that need not delay us here. Whatever the chronology or the provenance, anyone seeing these cards today must surely recognise that they are works of art. This is not surprising when one situates the artist in relation to his contemporaries in Italy: Botticelli (1445–1510); Leonardo Da Vinci (1452–1519); Michelangelo (1475–1564); Raphael (1483–1520), for instance. These cards are Early Renaissance works of art. Four of the original set have been lost. The Devil, the Tower, the Knight of Coins and the Three of Swords. They have since been replaced.

This earliest set is known as the Visconti-Sforza deck. Francesco Sforza, who died in 1466, was the owner. He married Bianca Maria Visconti, the only daughter of the Duke of Milan, thereby merging two important families. He hoped to succeed to the dukedom. However, after Duke Fillippo's death in 1447, Milan declared itself to be the Ambrosian Republic and dukes became redundant. Francesco, however, was having none of it. He proceeded to conquer the whole region city by city and eventually proclaimed himself Duke in 1550, adopting the Visconti family crest, which was a dove rising above its nest in the shape of a ducal crown, represented as the rising sun, which he added to his own: a lion with three interlocking rings. These telltale features appear on the cards, and allow us to identify them as his. We are not quite clear whether the cards were painted as a wedding present or as a celebration of his triumphal entry into Milan as Duke on 25 March. Whatever about these ancillary details, the set represents the first tarot cards we have and their purpose was essentially ornamental and for entertainment. The imagery, however, and the symbolism are European and Christian.

The tarot cards, as such, may not have been invented in the fifteenth century. The idea might have come from somewhere else. Speculation points towards Islamic countries, and Ferrara in Italy is suggested as the port of entry, because of specific mention in Ferrarese records from 1442. Wherever they came from, they were in regular and general use as playing cards throughout Italy by the sixteenth century.

Cartomancy, or the use of the tarot cards for divinatory or occult purposes, only began in eighteenth-century France. Antoine Court de Gébelin (1725–1784), a French Protestant clergyman, also archaeologist and Freemason, held that the cards derived from 22 stones buried between the paws of the Sphinx, which in turn had been encoded by Egyptian priests to conceal esoteric religious doctrines. Egyptomania was rampant during his lifetime and this was probably the incentive for harnessing this Italian import to a hermetic doctrine supposedly devised in Egypt but in fact used much more innocently for game playing. His friend, the Comte de Mellet, elucidated this explanation, showing also how the cards linked to the Hebrew alphabet in another tradition of divination. Even more influential in the spread of such occult explanations of the tarot was Eliphas Lévi, whose birth name was Alphonse Louis Constant, formerly a Roman Catholic priest, who became a journalist and magician. Once such connections had been made by these inventive symbolists, it was an easy step towards further suggestive association. The Jewish Cabala has often been presented as a source for the cards, each of the trumps being associated with a letter of the Jewish alphabet. There is no proof whatever that any such cards existed in the Jewish mystical or esoteric tradition. All the evidence points to retrospective and often ingenious application by post-eighteenth century occultists. Many similar juxtapositions were later superimposed on such movements as Swedenborgianism, spiritualism, alchemy and astrology. The hijacking of the tarot cards for such purposes spread from France to England, and there, through the extraordinary custodianship of the Order of the Golden Dawn, spread throughout the world. This last esoteric society was indirectly responsible for the so-called Ryder-Waite pack of tarot cards. Since the 1880s this popular version has become almost universally accepted as the standard tarot deck. Since that time also, all tarot cards have been understood to form an essential part of the practice of magic and are known only as manifestations of the occult tradition.

I am not claiming to know where the tarot cards came from. They are, in some of their manifestations, works of art and come from the deeper creative layers of the human unconscious. What I am saying is that they are certainly not intrinsically evil, as many might hold, nor are they attributable to any of the ancient pre-Christian religions to which they have been traced by many ingenious but erroneous advocates. On the contrary, they are very beautiful and inspiring images that can be used as provocative and helpful spring-boards to meditation. The purpose of this book is to show how this can be done.

Two scholarly books on Tarotism have recently appeared. *A Wicked Pack of Cards* in 1996 and *A History of the Occult Tarot, 1870–1970* in 2002.[2] These books were researched by an Australian anthropologist, Donald Laycock, an art historian, Ronald Decker, and the Wykeham Professor of Logic at Oxford from 1979 to 1992, Michael Dummett. Such credentials could hardly be more impeccable! The first of these books studies the esoteric use of the tarot cards from the first available evidence of such use in France up to the early twentieth century. All the major packs published during this period, both esoteric and divinatory, are presented and discussed. Biographical data on the major theorists, their thought, their sources and their symbolic maps, are provided and analysed. Misconceptions and misrepresentations are definitively repudiated. The second book provides a comprehensive and thorough chronicle of the whole history of the tarot cards. The conclusions are that, far from originating in Asia or Africa, the entire Middle East had to wait until the twentieth century to be introduced to the tarot. There is no evidence of their existence outside of Italy at any time before the fifteenth century. Nothing supports the theory that they originated in Egypt. Neither can their Jewish or Muslim origins be sustained scientifically. These authors are quite clear that in eighteenth-century France 'an Italian import formerly used for humble game playing, devoid of esoterism' was hijacked for the purposes of occult cartomancy. They also claim that 'when these facts are acknowledged, the migration of Tarotism becomes sensible and clear.'3 It went from France to England, where the French theories were applied by the Golden Dawn. It was also through French influence that the occult tarot spread eastwards. The cards have been associated with the so-called 'gypsies', the wandering Romany people. It is possible that they used them for divinatory and fortune-telling purposes from an early date. However, since their entry to Europe happened in the fifteenth century, their use of the cards does not shed light on the origins of the cards themselves.

Obviously those who use the tarot cards for occult or divinatory purposes will scorn scientific or historical research as an instrument too crude to detect the origins of their magical trade. The tarot cards could have been directly inspired by any particular spirit at any particular time. The important point being made here is that all the claims made in the past for historical attachment to one particular culture or another are bogus. The cards did not originate from ancient Jewish or Egyptian culture. Wherever they came from, they are a comparatively recent phenomenon in Western European culture and, in the most authentic original versions discovered to date, they are imbued with Western European and Christian iconography and symbolism.

I labour this point because it is necessary at least to detach these images from false defamation and infamous connections that make them obnoxious to many well-meaning people who are thereby deprived of one of the most unique and idiosyncratic European aids to guided meditation and spiritual endeavour.

The particular cards that are used as illustrations in this book are the so-called Marseilles Deck. These have no spiritual or historical significance, which would give them precedence over the plethora of available decks that have been spawned the world over since their creation. Neither the fact that certain contemporary cartomancers have designated them as the authentic orthodox pack, nor that others believe the port of Marseilles to have been the harbourer of secret wisdom imported from elsewhere and encoded in these cards, influence this choice. Whatever their origin, these cards remain the most artistically striking, starkly symbolic and uncluttered version in existence. Their value as icons is intrinsic to their artistry. They come from the deepest layers of the European unconscious and they bear the unmistakeable imprint of human theodicy imbued with Christian soteriology. It seems likely that the prototypes came from Milan and that both the numbering and ordering of the cards was derived from this identifiable source, even though there were other versions and combinations extant. Italy is the birthplace, as it was for so many archetypal European manifestations, of the spirit.

The discovery of an eleventh-century stone sculpture in the Basilica of St Sernin near Toulouse that resembles card 21 of the major arcana of the Marseilles deck does not prove that the cards must be at least as old. The influence could easily have been reversed: the artists of Marseilles who had the job of composing a particular deck could have been inspired by local sculpture and imagery. The important fact is that by 1760 the particularly striking iconography of this pack became established. Marseilles, since its foundation 2,600 years ago, has always been a major port open to influence from the East. Even Mary Magdalene was believed to have arrived there to initiate Christianity in the region. There has been no shortage of glitterati in the visitors' book since the town was established. Any one of these could have been a model for the original artists who designed the cards. This does not mean that the figures or the symbolism presented had any other than a Western European archetypal shape.

We know, of course, that playing cards as such were in existence long before this particular set was designed. In 1369 cards were forbidden by royal interdict throughout the kingdom of France. This ban seems to have been less from religious motivation than from sociological concern about inroads which addiction to the game made into public service and other duties. The fourteenth-century monks of the Abbey of St Victor in Marseilles were forbidden to play cards in the cloister. The Abbey statutes for 1337 forbid the playing of 'paginae', which were presumably paper cards. This moratorium, which has never been revoked and which also finds its way into many ecclesiastical condemnations, seems to have been provoked by excess and malpractice of a social rather than an occult nature. Such games were an absorbing fashion among the nobility and not suitable therefore in a monastic regime of poverty and hard work. Such would seem to have been the motivation for prohibition, not because the cards involved magical practices.

The invention of printing made it possible to mass-produce the cards. In 1638 the Master Cartiers of Marseilles were officially authorised by the King to reproduce these particular cards. Over a million packs were printed in the seventeenth century, of which only three survive. Cards used for entertainment purposes were disposable, as they are today. This industry became centralised, a monopoly seems to have been established, and in 1930 Paul Marteau produced what he regarded as a definitive edition, incorporating the best of all the diverse varieties in existence. These he called 'The Ancient Tarot of Marseilles'. The genealogy of the tarot cards, therefore, is as follows in summary:

1. The first cards we know date from 1450 and are found in Italy.
2. Up to 1680 the cards were European and Christian in their iconographic symbolism.
3. In 1760 we find the first specific iconography of the Marseilles deck.
4. In 1930 Paul Marteau of the Grimaud family established the colour codes as we find them here. The printing houses of this family have issued the cards and maintained the copyright to this day.

People are alarmed, amazed, convinced, by the accuracy with which their futures can be outlined and their personalities sketched by so-called experts who read the tarot cards. Let us begin with a statement of fact: Anyone who tells you what the future is going to be is telling you a lie. There is no future laid out like a map. The future is what we make it. Of course, we can be told, and some are better than others at surmising what is most likely to happen if we go on being the way we are, and others around us do likewise. The tarot cards cannot foretell the future. No one can foretell the future. It doesn't take a genius to know that people are going to die, fall in love, make fortunes, split up, move house, change job, in every month of the new century. People who predict such things have no vision of what is about to happen, they know that you are a human being, they sense your personality, they absorb your psychic energy, some more sensitively than others, and they 'prophesy' about your future. Whatever they say that has no relevance or doesn't come to pass is forgotten; anything that rings true, or that corresponds to what happens to you later, is often exaggerated and afforded significance out of all proportion.

These cards are evocative images, or symbols, which portray in archetypal form an inner reality that is common to all of us as human beings, and yet peculiar to each of us at every moment of our lives. This is why they can be used to 'predict' what is about to happen to us. There is a limited number of things which can happen to any or every human being in the course of any or every day of our lives: we are going to meet someone 'significant' (who isn't? Every person we meet is potentially our 'significant other'); we are going to meet up with death in some shape or form; we are going to achieve some goal; we are going to 'fall in love'; we are going to have an accident; we are going to come in for some good/bad fortune. But when these inevitabilities have been predicted, they suddenly take on the aura of prophecy, especially when aligned with the particular unfolding of our ordinary lives. The normal becomes paranormal because it has been pointed out as predestination. People we meet are enlarged and invested with significance; our amorous impulses are primed and ready to greet the next post-person who knocks at the door. The music of what happens becomes the orchestrated fanfare of the wedding, funeral or prize-giving march, which we have prerecorded, with original variations on the well-worn theme, courtesy of our psychic.

The future can only be shaped from whatever already exists, from the fairly predictable set of options which each one of us is.

Let me examine an often quoted example: the Titanic. In the early 1860s Edward Harland and Gustav Wolff opened a shipyard in Belfast. Harland and Wolff became the greatest and most advanced shipyard in the world. The company was able to accommodate the Titanic, which was designed and built by William Pirne's firm. This ship, at the time, was the biggest moving object ever constructed. As one commentator describes, the Titanic was 'the hoped-for trump card in the technological race to control Atlantic travel'. 'Promoted as unsinkable even as the first reports of her destruction arrived in

Halifax, Titanic brought the term "floating palace" into the English language.'

At the same time as the opening of Harland and Wolff, on 30 September, 1861, to be precise, a man called Morgan Andrew Robertson was born. He left school at sixteen, and from 1877–1886 he served in the Merchant Marine service where he eventually became First Mate. He left the service and apprenticed himself to a jeweller. His eyesight did not allow him to continue this career so, at the age of thirty-six, he began to write. According to his own account he had great difficulty writing and even greater difficulty earning his living in this profession. He wrote sea stories mostly, relying on his own experience of this life and the public's taste for adventure, especially adventure in the newly developed steam-ships, which increased the danger at the same time as they expanded horizons for travellers. Robertson wrote over 200 short stories, and published fourteen books between 1896 and his death at the age of 54 in March 1915.

In 1898, fourteen years before the Titanic was sunk, he wrote a story called *Futility*. It begins: 'She was the largest craft afloat and the greatest of the works of men. In her construction and maintenance were involved every science, profession, and trade known to civilisation.'[4] 'With nine compartments flooded the ship would still float, and as no known accident of the sea could possibly fill this many, the steamship Titan was considered practically unsinkable... Unsinkable – indestructible, she carried as few boats as would satisfy the laws.'[5] 'Seventy-five thousand tons – dead-weight – rushing through the fog at the rate of fifty feet a second, had hurled itself at an iceberg.'[6] The ship, carrying about 3,000 passengers, sinks at midnight in the month of April. Thirteen people survive.

Obviously when the real Titanic met a similar fate on 12 April, 1912, the prophetic quality of the book was noticed and a revised edition was published, with a new title: *The Wreck of the Titan, Or Futility*. The question then is: did this author have a preview of the future and was his text a prophecy of the disaster to come? Many people believe so. And in the same way many card-sharps claim to be able to tell, through the tarot cards, what is going to happen to their clients. And many make a living from it. Morgan Robertson was also trying to make his living from his stories. It is true that there were many similarities between the fictional Titan and the Titanic; nevertheless most of these are easily explainable. It also should be noted that the author and his publisher for the second edition of the story, which they produced after the Titanic had sunk, changed at least two of the details to make it look even more like a prophecy. They changed the tonnage and the horsepower of the Titan from 40,000 to 75,000 and from 45,000 to 70,000 respectively. And who would blame either for trying to capitalise on a strange, not to say ominous, co-incidence. However, from our point of view it is important not to be taken in by such claims. Both the story and the invention of the Titanic itself were works of the human imagination. Both came from a third source: the unconscious.

It is interesting to note that Morgan Robertson, whose imagination was, from an early age, captured by the sea, believed that he had invented the periscope. He knew that almost magic powers could be accorded to a submarine that could stay underwater and at the same time hoist to surface level an eye that could see, so he spent many years of his life inventing such a valuable asset. He did, in fact, do so, but when he went to patent his invention he was told that a French novelist had already described such a phenomenon in a work of fiction predating his own scientific discovery.

The sewing machine was 'discovered' in 1841 by two different people at the same time, Elias Howe in America and Barthélemy Thimonnier in France. One of these inventors describes his experience. He had made all the connections necessary: the shuttle to carry thread powered by a treadle and finally the needle itself. However, he could not get his machine to work. Eventually, he had a nightmare. In his dream he is about to be sacrificed by a group of highly painted savages armed with spears. As one of these is about to pierce his heart, he notices that a human eye is painted under the head of the weapon. He wakes up. Then he understands that for his new invention to work, the thread must be through the head or the top of the needle rather than through the end of it which is how one sews normally. So, the unconscious conspires with the conscious mind when we enter the realms of creativity and imaginative genius. And the outcome of most events, along with the solution to most problems, are already present in our unconscious because they are nothing more than the connection of various elements already given in the universe.

Anyone naming a ship or a novel in which the largest vessel imaginable is involved, must at some point come up against the mythical story of the Titans. These were the children of Heaven (Uranus) and Earth (Gaea). There were twelve titans, of whom one was the ocean (Oceanus). They rebelled against their father at the instigation of their mother and started the battles known as Titanomachia. The largest moon of Saturn is called Titan, and any dictionary will give a definition of the word as 'having huge or colossal stature'. So, the name of the ship that Morgan Robertson dreamed up, and the name of the one designed at Harland and Wolff get no big marks for originality, nor is the similarity of these names any proof of prophetic insight.

There are at least nineteen documented cases of people who had what are called 'precognitive' glimpses of the sinking of the Titanic itself. Some were passengers who drowned, some were would-be passengers who survived, others were not directly involved with the ship. We shall be exploring this phenomenon in a later chapter. For the present, this quotation from the physicist David Bohm (1917–1992) will be sufficient:

When people dream of accidents correctly and do not take the plane or ship, it is not the actual future that they were seeing. It was merely something in the present which is implicate and moving toward making that future. In fact, the future they saw differed from the actual future because they altered it. Therefore I think it's more plausible to say that, if these phenomena exist, there's an anticipation of the future in the implicate order in the present. As they used to say, coming events cast their shadows in the present. Their shadows are being cast deep in the implicate order.[7]

Artists have a capacity to read the significance of the present in terms of what it will produce in the future when its implication has been unfolded. They read the signs of the times and understand the significance of what is happening before their eyes in a way that is much more prophetic and insightful than any premonition. Following our present example, one work of art created two years after the sinking of the Titanic used this event to describe a whole century of such crashing and sinking. The poem which Thomas Hardy wrote in 1914, the year when the first world war began, suggests that the sinking of the Titanic on the night of 14 April, 1912, was the event which summarised the recklessness and mechanised slaughter upon which humankind was about to embark. The Titanic told in miniature what the Great War would tell in a major key and what the twentieth century would play out on the widest screen ever invented. The Titanic mesmerised that entire century. Art, if we are prepared to give the cinema such a name, seems to have ended the century with the same striking image: some two billion people, the largest audience ever to have witnessed any event in the past, watched the film *Titanic* which captured the imagination of the whole world.

Here is Hardy's poem:

The Convergence of the Twain
Lines on the loss of the 'Titanic'

I
In a solitude of the sea
Deep from human vanity,
And the Pride of Life that planned her, stilly couches she.

II
Steel chambers, late the pyres
Of her salamandrine fires,
Cold currents thrid, and turn to rhythmic tidal lyres.

III
Over the mirrors meant
To glass the opulent
The sea-worm crawls – grotesque, slimed, dumb, indifferent.

IV
Jewels in joy designed
To ravish the sensuous mind
Lie lightless, all their sparkles bleared and black and blind.

V
Dim moon-eyed fishes near
Gaze at the gilded gear
And query: 'What does this vaingloriousness down here?' ...

VI
Well: while was fashioning
This creature of cleaving wing,
The Immanent Will that stirs and urges everything

VII
Prepared a sinister mate
For her – so gaily great –
A shape of Ice, for the time far and dissociate.

VIII
And as the smart ship grew
In stature, grace, and hue,
In shadowy silent distance grew the Iceberg too.

IX
Alien they seemed to be:
No mortal eye could see
The intimate welding of their later history,

X
Or sign that they were bent
By paths coincident
On being anon twin halves of one august event,

XI
Till the Spinner of the Years
Said 'Now!' And each one hears,
And consummation comes, and jars two hemispheres.

The poem has many possible interpretations. At the beginning
of the century, for Hardy, the loss of the Titanic symbolised the
clash between the old world of nature and the new world of
science and industrialisation. Many of his novels treat of the
destruction of rural England and its old methods of farming, as
it were, by hand, with the introduction of machinery and
industrial technology. The Titanic was a microcosm of society
in 1912 and it represented the triumph of science and of human
technology over the destructive forces of nature in terms of the
sea. This ship was unsinkable according to its Belfast makers.
But such machines also introduced a kind of carnage and
destruction, whether through organised warfare or haphazard
accident, never before suffered or witnessed by the human
species. The Victorians had a morbid fascination with train
crashes and shipwrecks, which became the subject of so many
paintings and poems.

At the end of the twentieth century, another interpretation became possible. The ship represented successful and glamorous progress along the surface of the ocean. The iceberg represents that part of ourselves, our lives, which lies buried beneath our consciousness. The discovery of the 'night-world' of the unconscious, at about the same time as Hardy was writing this poem, revealed that human beings were far more complex and extensive than science and medicine had supposed up to that time. The iceberg has often been used as an image of the unconscious, that vast continent beneath the ordinary everyday surface of our lives, to which we gain access through our dreams and which we ignore at our peril, because: 'as the smart ship grew/ In stature, grace, and hue,/ In shadowy silent distance grew the Iceberg too.' The sinking of the Titanic was the destruction of a confident world of human progress on the surface of the material world, and the revelation of an underworld which needs other kinds of wisdom and techniques to gain access to it sufficiently to prevent it from taking over.

What I am suggesting in this book is that the tarot cards provide such a technique and, if used meditatively, such wisdom. They give us a map of at least one part of the unconscious world, and introduce us to some of the *dramatis personae*.

CHAPTER THREE

YEATS, TAROT, AND THE GOLDEN DAWN

Villiam Butler Yeats' (1865–1939) interest, not to say
obsession, with finding some system of belief went
back to his childhood.[1] His father was a highly
intelligent and sensitive agnostic who succeeded in
undermining any possibility of his son's finding satisfactory
religious insertion into the Christian denominations available at
the end of the nineteenth century in Ireland or England. Yeats
himself felt that he could not live without religion and so he set
about examining this phenomenon with all the dedication,
scepticism and inventiveness that characterised his exhaustive
research in most areas in which he became interested. He
turned to mysticism and the occult, founding the Dublin
Hermetic Society in June 1885, when he was twenty years of age.

It is hard to understand why students of Yeats have
refused to take him seriously at this level. He is acknowledged
as a poet, a dramatist, a senator, but regarded by many as either
a charlatan or a carpet-bagger in the area of mysticism. His
religious path took him through the Esoteric Section of the
Theosophical Society in London from 1888 to 1890, to
membership of the Hermetic Order of the Golden Dawn from
1890 to 1923. He was also an Associate Member of the Society
for Psychical Research from 1913 to 1928. He claimed in
Autobiographies that it was this journey that allowed him to
break away from his father's influence. And, indeed, one of the
more striking proofs of the seriousness of his endeavours is
supplied in reaction to attempts his father made to put an end
to his mystical pursuits. John Butler Yeats was afraid that his
son's poetry and his health would be damaged by the amount of

energy and time he was devoting to magical studies, so he asked John O'Leary, whom his son admired, to intervene. O'Leary's protegé replied in words that should really suffice to vindicate his seriousness:

> I chose to persist in a study which I decided deliberately four or five years ago to make, next to my poetry, the most important pursuit of my life.

> The mystical life is the centre of all that I do and all that I think and all that I write ... and I have always considered myself a voice of what I believe to be a greater renaissance – the revolt of the soul against the intellect – now beginning in the world.[2]

As well as the official association with various orders and societies, there was also Yeats' interest, developed from early childhood, in Irish folklore, the pre-Christian religious beliefs of his country of birth, and the living tradition of tangible and oral celebration of another world aligned to and intermingled with this one, which was part of the living culture of the countryside where he grew up.

I am taking it as now established, through works such as those of George Mills Harper[3] and Kathleen Raine[4], and more recently and more definitively by the first volume of Roy Foster's long awaited biography, entitled *The Apprentice Mage*,[5] that Yeats did, in fact, take very seriously his work in the area of mystery, magic and mysticism, that he was a very religious person:

> I was unlike others of my generation in one thing only. I am very religious, and deprived by Huxley and Tyndall, whom I detested, of the simple-minded religion of my childhood, I had made a new religion, almost an infallible Church of poetic tradition ... passed on from generation to generation by poets and painters with some help from philosophers and theologians.'[6]

He joined the Hermetic Order of the Golden Dawn in 1890. In contrast to most other orders of this kind, from the very beginning women were admitted as full members. The Order had been founded two years earlier in 1888 by William Wynn Westcott (1848–1925) and Samuel Liddell Mathers (1854–1918), who was married to Moina Bergson, sister of the famous philosopher Henri Bergson. All such orders are based on the belief of its members that they are the inheritors of a secret tradition which has been passed down through the centuries and which originates with some otherwordly source. Westcott was determined to supply such credentials to his new order and he claimed to be in possession of a very ancient secret manuscript containing wisdom dating at least from a fourteenth-century Christian Rosencreutz, to whose brotherhood his order belonged. However, those entering the Order of the Golden Dawn believed that the wisdom he transmitted was even more ancient than this, and rumour had it that Moses himself had been one of those initiated to it.

The Order, which lasted for about ten years of flourishing existence before going into dispersal and decline, was extraordinarily convincing and successful. Decker and Dummett[7] attribute this success to the unlikely combination of the strengths and weaknesses of the two founders. They give the example of a game of Bridge, where two partners have hands of cards neither of which is impressive in itself but which 'fit together so perfectly as to yield an irresistible slam'. These two people came together to provide the perfect magic lantern or Aladdin's cave in which W. B. Yeats could find the growth for his spiritual imagination, which no other 'order' could have provided. He joined at the age of 25, and left 33 years later, having experienced it at its best and at its worst. Westcott and Mathers, 'both inadequate human beings, neither equipped with talents that would have seemed in any way outstanding', combined between them to produce 'a result of genius' (HOC, 91). This 'result of genius' was the compilation of a compendium of Magic, both in theory and in practice, which, in fact, has become the primary source for most occult societies which have developed and proliferated throughout the world since then.

Eventually both Westcott and Mathers were shown up, with hindsight, to have been imposters and deceivers. Whether conscious or unconscious from the beginning is unclear in the case of Mathers, less convincingly so in the case of Westcott. The founding documentation, the most decisive of which was known as the Cypher Ms, was a hoax. Whether either or both were aware of this fact, it revealed itself to be such before the endgame of the order. Later scholarship revealed that the manuscript could not have existed before 1842, as it makes reference to books published only in that year. But by the time this fraud had become common knowledge Mathers had got himself too embroiled, and his absolute authority was too heavily invested in such authenticity, to admit that he had been duped. He claimed that he had known about Wescott's duplicity but that he himself had had his own private communication with 'the secret chiefs' of the order. These, in the end, established him as the only authentic source of the order's validity.

He eventually persuaded himself that the incarnation of that mediatrix of his authority, his channel of communication with the other world, had arrived in Paris in the person of Mrs Horos (Editha Salomon). She was an American confidence trickster, now accompanied by her fourth husband, Theo Horos (Frank Dutton Jackson), who had spent most of her life swindling the gullible in her guise as a spiritualistic medium. Mathers confided in her all the arcana of the order, supposed to have been kept secret from non-members. These were later revealed publicly in a scandalous court case in London, where Mr and Mrs Horos were convicted and sentenced to penal servitude. Their crime was seducing people of wealth and using the Golden Dawn rituals 'borrowed' from Mathers to initiate these into 'the order of Theocratic Unity', which involved eventually being raped, if necessary, by Mr Horos.

Among the major secrets revealed to the adepts of the order, under the severest injunctions never to tell these to anyone else, was the meaning of the tarot trump cards and their connection with the Hebrew alphabet. Only those in the order who attained the grade of Practicus could be trusted with this secret knowledge, which must never be disclosed to an uninitiated person. After the court case involving the Horos couple, this secret doctrine became common knowledge for anyone who cared to read about it in the scandal columns of the daily press.

Probably the most lasting, popular, and vernacular translation of this hidden meaning of the tarot trumps was the set of cards which eventually issued from the Golden Dawn indirectly. These have become known as the Rider-Waite deck and have since then almost replaced the Marseilles cards as the standard pack for Tarotists.

Arthur Edward Waite (1857–1942), with the publisher Rider & Co., produced the first set of tarot cards in English. He asked Pamela Colman Smith (1878–1951) to design the cards under his instruction, and these were later coloured by Mary Hanson-Roberts. Although Pamela Smith was not a great artist, she was genuinely imaginative and had a style that suited the commission. She was deeply influenced by William Butler Yeats, and at his instigation she joined the Golden Dawn in 1901. The cards, which carry no reference to her important contribution, owe to her a significant debt both for their imaginative symbolism and for their immediate and lasting popularity.

In a letter to Sturge Moore (27 May, 1926) Yeats declared that what Whitehead called the 'three provincial centuries' were over. The Western world had been hypnotised by a myopic reading of the universe and now 'Wisdom and Poetry return'. And these are two different things, which are listed in order of importance. He also believed that Ireland had a special role to play in ushering in this new order. Being on the edge of Europe and escaping many of the influences which shaped the mainland for better and for worse, it had preserved in its language, its people, its folklore and even in the psychic memory of its natural landscape, a Celtic world-view, a druidic religious sensibility which would help the new reign of wisdom and poetry to refertilize the arid desert of rationalistic empiricism. He was interested in creating a Celtic Order of Mysteries which would 'select its symbols from all the things that had moved men "through many, mainly Christian, centuries"'.[8] Maud Gonne was sympathetic to this desire. 'He used her clairvoyance to produce "forms that would arise from both minds." They worked through visions to create "a symbolic fabric".' Yeats seemed to have been aware at all times of his dependence upon others for his own mystical life. He was something of an orphan in the spiritual realm and did not possess the self-contained visionary faculty that others like AE, Blake and MacGregor Mathers embodied.

On the other hand, he did have a very healthy scepticism and a desire for rigorous examination of all such spiritual phenomena, which made him one of the most interesting and sympathetic witnesses for those on the outside. He was thrown out of the Esoteric Section of the Theosophical Society in London for being too sceptical and questioning their most sacred truths. He also was critical of AE's lack of discrimination and his unquestioning acceptance of every spiritual manifestation. The story of his association with the Order of the Golden Dawn is probably the most revealing from the point of view of his spiritual life.

The painstaking research of George Mills Harper[9] presents a crazy, sometimes hilarious, account of the life of this unusual order. How Yeats could have devoted so much of his time and energy to its perpetuation is an important question. Part of the answer is that not having within himself the visionary faculty, he had to rely on those who did, and submit himself to a discipline, an obedience and a ritual which would allow him access to the realities he knew were all-important. He found such a leader in MacGregor Mathers, and in the

Order of the Golden Dawn, Yeats tells us: 'I learned a practice, a form of meditation that has perhaps been the intellectual chief influence on my life up to perhaps my fortieth year.'[10]

Mathers was given important financial support by Miss Annie Horniman, also a member of the Order. This formidable lady has been pithily described by Norman Jeffares:[11] 'A Quaker and a feminist, ... a middle-aged middle-class dissenting spinster. She wore a dragon jewel of oxidised silver which she said was a likeness of herself.' She had a vested interest in Yeats also, supporting his new Abbey Theatre project until he decided to stage Shaw's play, *The Shewing up of Blanco Posnet*, though it had been banned in England, especially as he refused to close doors on the night the King of England died in a gesture of sympathy. She and Lady Gregory loathed one another with what has been described as the particular zest reserved for competing patrons. She was Yeats' staunchest ally in the Golden Dawn crisis.

This crisis has all the fantastic drama and colourful eccentricity of a comic opera. It resulted in the dismissal of Mathers from the Order on 21 April, 1900. Yeats then found himself not only 'fatherless', but also the only person left in the order who could assume responsibility for continuing it in the absence of the great guru. The letters that he addressed to the members of the order at this crucial and formative time express most profoundly his own position and belief.

Mathers was not expelled for having too little spiritual authority; it was a case of his exercising too much. He was claiming to be the only filter of spiritual energy in the organisation and was demanding total and blind obedience from all his followers to the point of megalomania. He had moved to Paris and was trying to exercise autocratic dictatorship from this distance. He expelled Miss Horniman for insubordination and was demanding total submission from all other members, when the mutiny occurred. The members in London set up a committee to investigate accusations made against the leader, and Mathers was summoned by this committee, which included Yeats, to come personally and account for his stewardship. Mathers, who refused to recognise the committee, sent as his representative a person who can be described as Yeats' *Doppelgänger*, the incarnation of all the caricatures and accusations of poseur, charlatan and literary fop, which his enemies and friends were inclined to spread about him. Aleister Crowley, self-styled Laird of Boleskine and Abertaff, broke into the Order's meeting rooms in London, 'in Highland dress, a black mask over his face and a plaid thrown over his head and shoulders, an enormous gold or gilt cross on his breast, and a dagger at his side'.[12] He seized the property on the authority of Mathers. The members had to call a constable to have him removed and then had the locks changed on the doors of the Adepti's vault in 36 Blythe Road, Hammersmith.

Crowley believed himself to be a prophet of Antichrist, under the sign of the Apocalyptic 'Great Beast' and the number 666. He and Yeats shared a belief that a Second Coming was at hand. Crowley wrote many volumes of poetry and resented Yeats' dismissal of these as bad verse, but much of their symbolic imagery would seem to come from a common fund of esoteric tradition. 'In an unsympathetic mood' Kathleen Raine suggests,[13] 'we might see in the purple style of Yeats' *bête noire*, Aleister Crowley, a caricature of Yeats' own.' In George Moore's fictional biography, Yeats is presented as 'a Finnish sorcerer, a subaltern soul, a literary fop ... a man of excessive appearance ... a long black cloak drooping from his shoulders, a soft black sombrero on his head, a voluminous black silk tie flowing from his collar, loose black trousers dragging untidily over his long, heavy feet and he was like "a rook, a crane, a Bible reader," or "a great umbrella forgotten by some picnic party".'[14]

On the one hand, there is the fallen idol, whom Yeats must have helped to write at least some of the Golden Dawn rituals,[15] and on the other there is the living caricature of what he might become without discernment, correction and guidance. Between these two archetypes there is the inevitable collapse of the Order if Yeats does not intervene. *Demon est*

Deus Inversus, Yeats' title in the Order (Miss Horniman
addressed him in her letters as 'My Dear Demon'), had to step
into MacGregor's shoes in a way which forced him to become
what he never really believed himself to be – a spiritual leader.

The important documentary sources here are letters
that Yeats wrote to the other members of the Order of the
Golden Dawn 'On the Present Crisis' in the first half of 1901.[16]
He is trying to define the identity of the Order and, at the same
time, trying to identify his own religious belief. The departure
of Mathers has created a possible anarchy in the Order,
whereby individuals are seeking the 'freedom' to pursue their
own spiritual quest without guidance, criticism or correction
from any centralised hierarchical authority. The question is
about spiritual authority in the absence of a recognised and
established prophetic figure. Yeats is trying to replace the
authority of a 'father figure' by one which is invested in the
Order itself. Mathers was not an indispensable guru and
certainly not a God. He was 'a unifying figurehead rather than a
divine agent',[17] but his departure does not mean the
introduction of egalitarianism or libertarian democracy where
spiritual authority is concerned. Between totalitarian
infallibility on the one hand and individual autonomy on the
other, he places the 'ritualistic and symbolic means of attaining
union with (or in) divinity... A treading of a symbolic path, a
passage through a symbolic gate, a climbing towards the light
which it is the essence of our system to believe.'[18] This is as
good a description as we are likely to find of the way in which
the tarot cards can be used for spiritual purposes. Such words,
as Harper has so meticulously shown, also reveal the secret of
Yeats' attachment to the Golden Dawn. He believed in order,
authority and degree: his search for meaning in a chaotic
natural universe required a framework and a system. In his
father's world there was no 'other' reality, and self-expression
was the most important activity of the human being. Yeats
would be and should be a great poet; what else was there to
strive for? The idea that he would sacrifice this talent to some

superstitious servility was anathema to John Stuart Mills' 'disciple', and the son describes the violence of their disagreement: 'When I was twenty-three or twenty-four we began to quarrel... Once he threw me against a picture with such violence that I broke the glass with the back of my head.'[19]

The struggle between being a poet and being a mystic; between active pursuit of self-expression and passive receptivity of a larger, more inaccessible vocabulary; between obedient listening to the word of God and writing your own words, remained with Yeats until he broke away from the Golden Dawn. This strange preoccupation provoked much angry intervention on behalf of poetry from those like W.T. Horton, who felt that Yeats was squandering his genius on a 'spiritism and spiritistic investigation' that 'leads to nothing':

> To see you on the floor among those papers searching for an automatic script ... while round you sit your guests, shocked me for it stood out as a terrible symbol. I saw you as the man with the muck rake in "The Pilgrim's Progress" while above you your Beloved held the dazzling crown of your own Poetic Genius. But you would not look up and you went on with your grovelling.[20]

It almost seems as if the crisis which he experienced and analysed so painstakingly in the body politic of the Order of the Golden Dawn prefigured a similar realisation in his own life. The following description of the crisis in the Order contains elements similar to what later happened to himself:

> Sometimes the sphere of an individual man is broken, and a form comes into the broken place and offers him knowledge and power if he will but give it of his life. If he give it of his life it will form a swirl there and draw other forms about it, and his sphere will be broken more and more, and his will subdued by an alien will.[21]

In his own case, an elaborate explanation had to be devised to do full justice to the nature, the authority, the integrity and the source of the revelation that was given to him, which he later formulated in his enigmatic work *A Vision*. Here again it is interesting to read his peroration to fellow members of the Golden Dawn:

> We have set before us a certain work that may be of incalculable importance in the change of thought that is coming upon the world. Let us see that we do not leave it undone because the creed of the triflers is being cried into our ears.[22]

The creed of the triflers is not only scientific rationalism but would include those who place poetry before mysticism. Yeats was very clear about his twofold duty. His strange task was to provide a new understanding of very ancient truths, an order of religion that found its being and its personality in symbolic rites and accurate ceremonial. It was a kind of Magic, but not in any way associated with Black Magic; it had no quarrel with the true Christian religion or its symbolism, if this is understood in the liturgical way of its mysteries, 'for there is but one life. Incarnate life, just in so far as it is incarnate, is an open or veiled struggle of life against life, of number against number, and of all numbers against unity'.[23] Yeats' major struggle was to preserve unity. He believed that by preserving unity and making it efficient:

> The Order will become a single very powerful talisman, creating in us, and in the world about us, such moods and circumstances as may best serve the magical life, and best awaken the magical wisdom. Its personality will be powerful, active, visible afar, in that all powerful world that casts downward for its shadows, dreams, and visions. The right pupils will be drawn to us from the corners of the world by dreams and visions and by strange accidents; and

the Order itself will send out Adepts and teachers, as well as
hidden influences that may shape the life of these islands.[24]

His approach to both the unconscious and the sacred was
idiosyncratic and ingenious; some would say absurd. From his
earliest years he believed in 'the practice and philosophy of
what we have agreed to call magic'.[25]

Yeats' belief in the *Anima Mundi* seems to have been
similar to C. G. Jung's description of a collective unconscious;
their notion of the shared undercarriage of our psyches, which
communicate and correspond through the medium of
symbols; their theories of 'persona' and 'mask'; and their
geometrical patterns described in terms of mandalas by Jung
and through diagrams in Yeats' *A Vision*, make it hard to
believe that they were unaware of and uninfluenced by one
another's work.

One of the major influences on Yeats' approach to the
sacred and to the unconscious was Sligo, the place where his
mother's family came from. This place had escaped from the
scientific materialism that the rest of Europe had allowed to
sanitise and disconnect its roots. The love for Sligo was not a
conscious philosophy, it was a gut feeling, reinforced and
identified by early exile to London:

> A poignant memory came upon me the other day while I
> was passing the drinking-fountain near Holland Park, for
> there I and my sister had spoken together of our longing for
> Sligo and our hatred of London. I know we were both very
> close to tears and remember with wonder, for I had never
> known any one that cared for such mementoes, that I
> longed for a sod of earth from some field I knew, something
> of Sligo to hold in my hand. It was some old race instinct
> like that of a savage.[26]

In an essay on 'The Celtic Element in Literature', Yeats
describes how 'once every people in the world believed that

trees were divine, and could take a human or grotesque shape and dance among the shadows'.[27] Such a world-view brought with it an attitude and a contact with the unconscious and the sacred:

> Men who lived in a world where anything might flow and change, and become any other thing; and among great Gods whose passions were in the flaming sunset, and in thunder and the thunder-shower, had not our thoughts of weight and measure. They worshipped nature and the abundance of nature, and had always, as it seems, for a supreme ritual that tumultuous dance among the hills or in the depths of the woods, where unearthly ecstasy fell upon the dancers, until they seemed the gods or the godlike beasts, and felt their souls overtopping the moon; and, as some think, imagined for the first time in the world the blessed country of the gods and of the happy dead. They had imaginative passions because they did not live within our own strait limits, and were nearer to ancient chaos, every man's desire, and had immortal models about them.[28]

This 'religious' attitude or 'habit', formed at the earliest period of Yeats' life, had two dispositive causes. The first was the religious vacuum created by his father's atheism; the second was the strongly pagan and primitive practices and beliefs of the local people in Sligo, who were his childhood playmates and surrogate family. Their 'Catholicism' was a thin veneer over a religion as old as the Sligo landscape. This landscape itself was a religious site, an incubating sanctuary pregnant with ecstasy-inducing symbols.

Temperamentally, Yeats was part of the Protestant ascendency class in Ireland. This was important for several reasons. It gave him a self-confidence and a sense of his own capacity to come to terms with the universe. He was born into an artistic family and from a comparatively early age was aware of his own position as one of the most gifted poets of his time.

Obviously, he had many experiences that undermined his belief in himself, from his early schooling in England where he was laughed at for being Irish, to his constant rejection by the women he loved. However, as compared with so many fellow Irish artists who were born on 'the wrong side of the tracks', Yeats had a superiority and what the ancient Romans would call an *hilaritas* which allowed him without scruple or qualm to invent his own religion.

In 1911, Evelyn Underhill first published her classic study *Mysticism*. In a chapter on 'Mysticism and magic' she describes the 'mistakes – in ecclesiastical language, the heresies – into which men have been led by a feeble, a deformed, or an arrogant mystical sense':

> The number of these mistakes is countless; their wildness almost inconceivable... It seems as though the moment of puberty were far more critical in the spiritual than it is in the physical life: the ordinary dangers of adolescence being intensified when they appear upon the higher levels of consciousness... Hence in every period of true mystical activity we find an outbreak of occultism, illuminism, or other perverted spirituality and – even more dangerous and confusing for the student – a borderland region where the mystical and psychical meet... In the youth of the Christian Church, side by side with genuine mysticism ... we have the arrogant and disorderly transcendentalism of the Gnostics: their attempted fusion of the ideals of mysticism and magic. During the Middle Ages and the Renaissance there are the spurious mysticism of the Brethren of the Free Spirit, the occult propaganda of Paracelsus, the Rosicrucians, the Christian Kabalists ... which make war upon Catholic tradition. In the modern world, Theosophy in its various forms is probably the most widespread and respectable representative of the occult tradition.[29]

The 'Catholic' tradition referred to here is not as narrow as might be supposed. Underhill eventually joined the Anglican tradition but engaged Baron Von Hugel until his death as her spiritual director. Von Hugel (1852–1925) was a Roman Catholic theologian, suspected by the authorities in his own church of 'modernist' tendencies, who wrote on mysticism. Yeats thought of him as 'sincere and noble' and refers to him in the poem 'Vacillation' (1932) as one whose views were sometimes similar to his own: 'Must we part, Von Hugel, though much alike, for we/ Accept the miracles of the saints and honour sanctity?' In the end, Yeats accepts that they must part, that however comforting Christianity might be, he is called to play a 'predestined part', for which Homer is the supreme example with his 'unchristened heart'. 'So get you gone, Von Hugel, though with blessings on your head.'

The kind of 'religion' that attracted Yeats was precisely the kind condemned in this passage by Evelyn Underhill. She even describes the difference between 'magic' and 'mysticism':

Magic is merely a system whereby the self tries to assuage its transcendental curiosity by extending the activities of the will beyond their usual limits... The fundamental difference between the two is this: magic wants to get, mysticism wants to give... In magic, the will unites with the intellect in an impassioned desire for supersensible knowledge. This is the intellectual, aggressive, and scientific temperament trying to extend its field of consciousness until it includes the supersensual world: obviously the antithesis of mysticism, though often adopting its title and style... Such philosophy is often wrongly called mysticism, because it tries to make maps of the countries which the mystic explores. Its performances are useful, as diagrams are useful, so long as they do not ape finality.[30]

Yeats would certainly have repudiated any such division between 'magic' and 'mysticism'. Not for him any mealy-mouthed humility or submissive passivity. His work *A Vision* is an attempt to effect the 'reconciliation of Paganism and Christianity'[31] and to articulate a new and total view of humanity in its ultimate connection with Being, Time and Eternity. His is an artist's intuitive grasp of those things which are 'in the air', which some refer to as the *Zeitgeist*. In his view there was a development occurring in humanity. We were approaching the end of an era of one kind of religiosity and about to enter another. He used every cultural and imaginative instrument at his disposal to give his readers an inkling of the revolution that he sensed was in store.

Yeats believed that the scientific materialism of his own age was a passing heresy. He saw his role as poet/prophet for a new era. He knew that this new era would need a spirituality that was worldwide and age-old. It would have to provide a metaphysics capable of dealing with not only the deep structures of our present life, but also with what precedes birth and follows death. Yeats was at all times preoccupied with the discarnate mode of being. In 'A general introduction for my work', written in 1937, he writes:

I am convinced that in two or three generations it will become generally known that the mechanical theory has no reality, that the natural and supernatural are knit together, that to escape a dangerous fanaticism we must study a new science; at that moment Europeans may find something attractive in a Christ posed against a background of Druidism, not shut off in dead history, but flowing, concrete, phenomenal. I was born into this faith, have lived in it, and shall die in it; my Christ, a legitimate deduction from the Creed of St Patrick as I think, is that Unity of Being Dante compared to a perfectly proportioned human body, Blake's 'Imagination,' what the Upanishads have named 'Self': nor is this unity distant and therefore intellectually understandable, but imminent, differing from man to man and age to age, taking upon itself pain and ugliness, 'eye of newt, and toe of frog.' Subconscious preoccupation with this theme brought me *A Vision*, its harsh geometry and incomplete interpretation.[32]

This faith, which Yeats calls 'Christian' and which he claims to have been 'born into', and which was the unconscious source of *A Vision*, is neither the Protestantism of his grandfather, who was Rector at Drumcliffe, nor the agnosticism of his father, nor the official version of Roman Catholicism (to which both Maude Gonne and Constance Markiewicz were converted in the later years of their lives). It was a Celtic Christianity, which he felt it his duty to excavate and articulate. The aspects of popular peasant Catholicism that interested him were precisely those regarded as superstition by his educated Protestant peers. Purgatory was an example of such belief. Yeats felt himself called to rescue the true Christ from centuries of distortion for which both Catholics and Protestants must take some blame. Yeats' 'predestined part' was that of 'resituating Christianity within the context of the perennial philosophy as a whole'. He also wished to reinvigorate those vestigial traces of an ancient druidic religion which survived in Ireland, mostly in an oral tradition transmitted by illiterate Irish-speaking people who were nominally part of an accommodating Catholicism.

He believed that true Christianity should be grafted to the indigenous religion of a country, that each country became a 'Holy Land' only when its imagination had been captured and its Old Testament led towards the expansive and comprehensive fulfilment of the new. Europe had no older or greater religious tradition than that embodied in the rites, the sites, the pilgrimages of pre-Christian, Celtic Ireland.

Byzantium, which symbolized for Yeats that perfect fusion of Christianity with the human imagination, in its early period was contemporaneous with St Patrick (396–469). The 'unity of being' within a 'unity of culture', which Yeats regarded as the goal of religious reconciliation, was evident in the Book of Kells and other art works of this period of Celtic culture.[33]

One of the major differences between this earlier Christianity and later manifestations of it, especially in the version being institutionalised in Ireland after independence, but also in various Protestant variations, was its capacity to integrate the sexual as a sacred mystery central to all life of whatever kind. The character of Crazy Jane in Yeats' imagination represents the Old Testament of the Celtic race crying out against the bishop, representing institutionalized religion, especially its contemporary Irish Catholic variety. Sexual prudery and puritanism were major enemies in Yeats' crusade for a more integrated and wholesome Christianity.

As a white Protestant male, Yeats enjoyed all the privileges of the ascendancy class and the psychological supremacy which made him equal if not superior to all opposition of whatever kind or period or from whatever quarter. He also enjoyed the company of a considerable number of highly talented, unusually liberated and intelligently self-assured women, many of whom led exciting, autonomous, fulfilling lives, quite different from their contemporaries in other countries, other religious backgrounds or social class. Yeats was by no means a feminist. He was as much a prisoner of the views on women prevalent at that time as most of his male contemporaries. However, he was highly sensitive, extravagantly appreciative of women in general, and obsessively devoted to a few in particular, and was privileged to be surrounded by exceptionally talented, educated and inspiring objects of his infatuation.

Most of his life was spent yearning for communion with about three women, who failed to respond as passionately to him as he would have hoped and who either did not really enjoy sexual relations at all or did not find satisfying such contact with him. However, at the age of 52, he married Georgie Hyde-Lees, who was 26 years younger than he was. A major source of both texts of *A Vision* was their relationship. *A Vision* was, at least initially, an attempt by Yeats to 'make sense of his sex life'. This and 'the beatific vision' were meant to be explained. However, neither of these ever became clear enough to him to allow this to happen. However, there is sufficient evidence at the moment to suggest that 'collaboration between the sexes was the enabling precondition of Yeats' achievement, and the topic of sexual love dominated his conversation with the spirits'.34

> In the 1925 version of *A Vision* Yeats lamented that Parmenidean abstraction had displaced the concerns that occupy 75 percent of the automatic script: "I have not even dealt with the whole of my subject, perhaps not even with what is most important, writing nothing about the Beatific Vision, little of sexual love" (AV[A]xii). The Vision papers reveal that the script was sexual both in its content ... and in the conditions of its reception. The power with which the spirits were able to communicate depended on the quantity and quality of Yeats' sexual relations with his wife.35

In other words, the source of Yeats' mystical writings is the blending of the collective unconscious with the corporate personality achieved by his wife and himself through satisfactory sexual communion, involving frequent intercourse which must include reciprocated orgasm. The fact that the channel for 'the voices' happened to be George and that the eventual text is philosophical and historical in content and geometrical in mode, should not blind us to the fact that what is being filtered is in essence from the unconscious, and the way it is being achieved is through the erotic and the personal. The sexual was 'the sixth sense' which could tune into the unconscious, creating the balance between creativity and sexuality which brought about 'unity of being'. Anne Saddlemeyer has provided the most convincing account of this common source of 'the script' which was communicated toW. B. and Georgie during so many hours of their married life.36 Such contact with the sacred is germane to a long tradition of mystical experience, which, from the book of Genesis, through the Song of Songs, to the writings of so many poets of mystical 'marriage', employs the image of male/female union to describe relationship with the divine.

Elizabeth Butler Cullingford sees the 'Supernatural Songs', which were written after Yeats had had an operation to restore his sexual potency, as 'the verses of a ribald iconoclast who is out to disturb musty piety, but is nevertheless serious about reconciling divine love with the natural emotion of human passion'.37 She also suggests that Yeats found in Indian Tantric philosophy 'the acceptance of sex as a road to divinity' and an affirmation of his own insistence upon 'an alliance between body and soul' which 'our theology rejects'.38

The script itself tells us that such 'revelation' requires 'Complete harmony between physical body intellect and spiritual desire – all may be imperfect but if harmony is perfect it is unity.' This 'equal balance' does not mean homogeneity at every level between partners, but it does require 'equal instinct and emotion'. The 'Wisdom of Two' requires sexual compatibility but at other levels a complete diversity of character and talent. It is as if the quite opposite genius of two extraordinary people needed to be fused in the heightened intensity of sexual union to allow both to be harnessed to the one creative purpose: the ensuing 'script'. The earliest notebooks of what their 'Instructors' tell them insist that 'sex and emotions must be alike (in harmony) mind and soul unlike in tendency and nature'. W. B. Yeats and his wife had the necessary combination between them to create a channel for the unconscious to emerge. Both were essential 'to get in touch with the pam [personal *Anima Mundi*] and the am [*Anima Mundi*]' and this could happen satisfactorily 'only if both people are being used by us' for 'when one only is used then we give only fragments'. '[W]e can't use you alone – must have you and medium *equally*.'39

Many have expressed irritation and surprise at the convoluted way in which Yeats camouflaged the origins of this later work. Whatever the reasons for this, and in my view they are understandable, given the personality of the man, the kind of society in which he lived, and the peculiar nature of these origins, the business of the critic is to understand these late works. And here, I believe, there can be no full understanding unless the phenomenon of *A Vision* is taken seriously, as it was by Yeats himself.

One example of this is the poem 'The Gift of Harun Al-Rashid', which explains the relationship between the poet's marriage and his initiation into the mysteries that constitute *A Vision*. It tells in hidden ways the story of his own marriage at the age of 52 with a young woman and how the ensuing ecstasy revealed through her was nothing less than the infrastructure of the universe. The intimacy of such personal contact is preserved through the exotic fantasia adopted to reveal it. The extraordinary world into which both he and his partner were introduced, through the everyday event of their sexual communion, is also conveyed by the unreal and antique nature of the story. Yeats had once said of Maud Gonne that his earlier poetry 'shadowed in a glass/ What thing her body was'; so he would claim that *A Vision* was like a cubist representation of the body of his wife. 'The Gift of Harun Al-Rashid' is possibly the nearest we might get to unscrambling that cubist encodement: 'Perhaps', as he said in 1934, 'now that the abstract intellect has split the mind into categories, the body into cubes, we may be about to turn back towards the unconscious, the whole, the miraculous.'[40]

Anne Saddlemeyer's painstaking biography of George Yeats has shown that she was, perhaps, the more important partner in the eventual achievement of the scripts. Yeats regarded himself as both the dispositive and the final cause of these revelations. He believed that it depended on him to make whatever use might be made of their common 'script'. 'As the script gained complexity, while George and the Instructors attempted to answer Willy's questions, and as the system itself expanded, more and more frequently the solutions turned on the astrological shorthand.'[41] The script as it finally emerged is probably much more beholden to George's contributions than it is to W. B.'s, although neither he nor she, nor for that matter any of the critics, would have believed this; nor would they have any interest in it – the only important thing about it was the effect it had on one of the great poets of the twentieth century. Yeats wrote in Capri in February 1925 when he was trying to summarise the meaning of *A Vision*: 'when the two halves of man can define each its own unity in the other as in a mirror, Sun in Moon, Moon in Sun, and so escape out of the Wheel.' This suggests, from the point of view of the Tarot cards, that it would be worth revisiting the automatic scripts in their entirety, not just to discover the images given to Yeats for his poetry, but for the contribution of both himself and George to the secret wisdom of the world.

Yeats was alive to this possibility and would have agreed with William James: 'The whole drift of my education goes to persuade me that the world of our present consciousness is only one out of many worlds of consciousness that exist.' The marriage of Yeats and George Hyde-Lees was much more of a sacred tryst than it was a romantic alliance. She was, in fact, the perfect partner to the apprentice mage, and his union with her was probably the most important energy in his life both as a person and as a poet. His connection with Maud Gonne and her daughter Iseult was far more absorbing and more stimulating in terms of literary gossip, romantic obsession and early poetry, but the deep sexual intimacy of his relationship with George was of a different order and became the source of whatever happiness he achieved, whatever mystical insight he gained, and whatever really great poetry and drama he wrote.

T. S. Eliot, in the first Annual Yeats Lecture delivered to the Friends of the Irish Academy at the Abbey Theatre in June 1940,[42] described Yeats' most enduring characteristic as a poet as the kind of 'impersonality', which 'out of intense and personal experience, is able to express a general truth; retaining all the particularity of his experience, to make of it a general symbol'. Eliot made no secret of his disdain for the 'craftmanship' of the early Yeats and for the kind of poetry which made him famous. He dismisses the Yeats of the Celtic twilight and calls him rather 'the Yeats of the pre-Raphaelite twilight'. He describes Yeats' posturing as the champion of Irishry and Celtic folklore as 'the western seas descried through the back window of a house in Kensington, an Irish myth for the Kelmscott Press'. But he is forced to admit that something happened to the later Yeats: 'He had to wait for a late maturity to find expression of early experience; and this makes him, I think, a unique and especially interesting poet.'

CHAPTER FOUR

TAROT: YOUR NUMBER IS UP

It is difficult for us to recognise the extent to which we have been led along the road outlined for us by the Greeks and the distance we are from the alternative route, the road not taken, of unconscious awareness, awareness of the unconscious. In fact, to a certain extent, it was only those marginalised from our education system who stumbled upon the alternative and who, in many cases, thereby became what we have termed great artists or geniuses of one kind or another. W. B. Yeats is a case in point. Listen to John Carey reviewing the first volume of Foster's biography of Yeats: 'Was he, you find yourself blasphemously wondering, really that intelligent?' and he lists the usual proofs of intellectual backwardness: 'He was substandard at school... He never learnt to spell: even as a grown man, simple monosyllables foxed him... His gullibility was fathomless. Mysticism and magic, to which he was introduced by the half-batty George Russell, occupied much of his waking and sleeping life. He believed he conversed with old Celtic gods and a copious ragbag of other supernaturals.'[1] What this critic fails to recognise is that there are different kinds of intelligence. Yeats' intelligence was essentially mythic. Such intelligence weaves its way through symbols and has a very different perspective on the universe to that of the scientist, for instance.

I wished for a world where I could discover this tradition perpetually, and not in pictures and in poems only, but in tiles round the chimney-piece and in the hangings that kept out the draught. I had even created a dogma: 'Because those imaginary people are created out of the deepest instinct of man, to be his measure and his norm, whatever I can imagine those mouths speaking may be the nearest I can go to truth'. When I listened they seemed always to speak of one thing only: they, their loves, every incident of their lives, were steeped in the supernatural.[2]

This last quotation is as good an introduction to the tarot cards as I have encountered: because these imaginary people are created out of the deepest instinct of humankind, to be our measure and our norm; they are as near as we can go to truth, and they are steeped in the supernatural. However, to be able to listen to what they say we have to reintroduce ourselves to a mythic way of thinking, which is the purpose of this chapter.

In Western European philosophy we were introduced by Auguste Compte to the idea that human intelligence had developed from a primitive mythic stage, through a medieval metaphysical stage, right up to the scientific rationalism that has so marked and transformed our world. This development was linear and rendered all stages that preceded it obsolete. There is no such evolutionary progress in a linear module, which casts off the previous in an advance towards the present, as a rocket might detach itself from the parts that launch it. Mythic intelligence is an essential kind of human understanding, and it is to our great impoverishment that our educational systems and our academic leaders treat it with such contempt.

It is difficult for us to step outside the spaceship and recognise just how programmed we are. Much in the same way that we recognise the overwhelming extent to which we are dependent upon electricity only when there is a power cut, we have to exercise our imagination almost violently to recognise the extent to which we are automised clones of an infrastructural grid laid down by the Graeco-Roman empires, and maintained with devastating tenacity by the guardians of academic protocol today.

Civilised societies of the twentieth century democratised the languages of reading and writing, for instance. These became the fundamental currency in the West. They also became the criteria for 'intelligence', as we see from the above assessment of W. B. Yeats by professors at Oxford in recent years. Only those who have fallen between the bars of the grid know the extent to which they are marginalised and deprived by illiteracy. We imagine that reading and writing are natural to us, whereas, in fact, they must be two of the most unnatural activities ever undertaken by creatures on this planet.

What is happening at this moment for you as a reader is a case in point. Between you and me at this moment in your life, is a page of print. These words form a code that, because you can read and I can write, allow me to communicate with you. The process is similar to drip-feeding. A vast multitude crowds towards one tiny entrance where one word appears at a time. I can only write one word at a time. I fill this page slowly and separately so that I can tell you word for word what is on my mind. You have become so used to gobbling up these units that you may not even notice the cumbersome technique necessary for you to eventually land these ideas in your mind. The further complication is this: because we have now been taught to read almost automatically, we tend to 'read' everything. This very complex skill, which we have all acquired, has warped our sensibility. We have turned ourselves into text maniacs, we 'read' our lives. So much so that if you ask a student in Europe these days, 'Where is Japan?' they are quite likely to tell you that it is on page 23 of their atlas or geography book.

When the cinema was invented at the beginning of the twentieth century, it was forced by our page-turning compulsion into a certain pattern that made early movies into novels for the screen. Images were never looked at or viewed for themselves; they were simply carriers of the story which rushed us headlong to the denouement. No one had time to stop and stare, we were taken on a roller-coaster ride from start to finish. We couldn't wait until we knew what happened in the end.

Nowadays we are beginning to return to the visual aspect. We are viewing pictures as things in themselves. We became visually impaired because we were no longer used to looking; we had been trained to read instead. So, when faced by an abstract painting or a piece of visual art we would want to know its 'meaning'. 'I can't see anything in it,' we'd say. 'What does red mean, what does blue signify, how do you read the different shades of green in this picture?' It never occurred to us that there might not be anything 'in' the picture apart from what it is in itself. All we had to do was look at it, or, indeed, let it look at us. But, we had lost our capacity to see anything except the small print. We were always looking for the subtitles so that we could read the film. People were quite satisfied if you told them that red meant blood, blue meant depression, green meant 'go ahead'. Nobody cared if the picture had been destroyed, or misinterpreted, or even betrayed by such translation; all that mattered was my literal explanation, the fact that I could read the surface satisfactorily.

Of course there is an advantage to having a common language. Science provides us with formulae that mean the same thing to every human being, no matter who or where you are. If you run 100 metres faster than your rival at the other side of the world, both you and your competitor have to agree about what a metre is. It used to be one ten-millionth part of a meridian that passes from the pole to the equator (reproduced in platinum on the official metre stick kept in Paris) until in October 1960 it was universally accepted to be 1,650,753.73 wavelengths of the orange-red light of krypton 86. So, it is standardised.

The trouble is that education of intelligence has also become standardised and only one variety has been valorised. Anything apart from the standard IQ has to fend for itself. Reading was, up to now, the standard way of sending information around the world. The new language of computerised technology may change this monocultural bias in the twenty-first century and impose a less demanding and more accessible common currency.

People of Western Europe in the twentieth century were not only able to read and write more or less instinctively, they translated everything that presented itself to them into this narrow network. We read music, art, cinema, life and love. Everything we did was a story, an alphabet, a grammar, a plot, a chapter, a closed book, a bestseller. We read and we wrote our lives. My diary was my day translated into linear modules of coherent literacy. When the new visual opportunity erupted in cinema, we killed it instantly by drip-feeding it models of literacy. Books on the screen, told in linear sequence, trampled the ubiquitous originality at our disposal into one long cable of monoglot consistency. It was as if the menu on our screen was to be one long reel of spaghetti because that was all we knew how to cook and all we cared to eat.

So, to 'read' the tarot cards we are going to have to unlearn a great deal, and to develop a long-lost technique of examining things visually, their shape, their colour, their placement, their proportionality, their symbolic weight. The other technique we have to develop in our reading of the cards is a more ancient and mysterious attitude towards numbers. Numbers too have undergone a debilitating homogenisation over the last two centuries. This reduction to the level of univocal figures parallels the spread of reading as the basic requirement in education. The development of the three Rs as the standard syllabus for all primary education lost us our capacity to see life as a mystery and prepared us to face it as a problem to be solved. The second set of cyphers to be learned was not as easy or as communicable as the first. Numeracy was not as widespread as literacy. Only certain minorities became expert and conversant.

People had to learn to read and write the language of measurement, if they were to understand modern science. This

meant a no-nonsense approach to numbers, which deprived
these of their magic. In the beginning we grunted and
extemporised verbally when trying to do our sums on the
turnips or the cattle we were counting or bartering. If human
beings did not have fingers, it is unlikely that we would have
learned to count. Our fingers are visual aids to counting. In its
initial stages, number was more of a manual than an
intellectual concept. The Latin word for a finger is *digitus*, from
which our term 'digit' and its adjective 'digital' derive. The fact
that we have five fingers on each hand, allowing us with natural
ease to count up to ten, introduces another familiar term,
which is the Latin word for ten, *decimus*, which introduces us
to the decimal system. It was the Arabs who invented this
'handy' system for counting, which took ten as its base. If I had
ten objects to account for I could cope. In at least one ancient
language the word for six is equivalent to the word for 'jump',
reminding our ancestors that after five they were required to
jump over to the other hand to continue the process of
calculation. In Euclidean geometry (the word 'geo-metry'
means 'measurement of the world') the assumptions are
explicit: the premises and conclusions derived from them are
formulated in words. Mathematics, which, as we surmised,
originated as a most natural way of counting using our hands
and sometimes our feet, had to undergo an excision of verbal
content to attain symbolic exactness. $5 + 5 = 10$ is an exercise
most of us can manage, it is short-hand for the ten fingers on
both our hands. However, five times that number is more
complicated and requires a kind of juggling, which was later
replaced with an easier, more manageable symbol. 'x' became
the sign or symbol for multiplication, so that:

$$5 \times 5 = 5 + 5 + 5 + 5 + 5$$

and

5 to the power of $5 = 5 \times 5 \times 5 \times 5 \times 5$
$(5+5+5+5+5)+(5+5+5+5+5)+(5+5+5+5+5)+(5+5+5+5+5)+(5+5+5+5+5)$

We are still within reach of our hands and our feet, digital calculation. But in Algebra (in Arabic the word *jabara* = reunite) the ties between words and operations and between objects and symbols are cut, so that the operations and symbols can be brought into closer mutual conformity. It is a language, but not connected to 'the real world', and it is restricted to defining relationships between signs and symbols. As the activity becomes more abstract and sophisticated, it is removed from the tangible world where most of us can find our feet, so to speak. We all know those people who have a gift for mathematics and those others who can't handle it at all. We're into a more rarefied world not accessible to everyone, as the symbolism of reading and writing are supposed to be.

However, as the mathematicians move further and further into rarefied abstraction, we all leave behind an understanding of and sensibility towards numbers, which is now regarded as primitive and obsolete. Number for our ancestors was a key to the secrets of the universe. Astrology supplied the belief that all aggregates with the same number were related: 4 seasons, 4 elements, 4 points of the compass, for instance; 7 days in a week, 7 planets. Each number had a hidden meaning that corresponded either to its own intrinsic qualities or to the things it designated. So, 1 designated unity, individuality, God; 2 was division or opposition; 3 was family, trinity; 4 was stability, matter; 7 was totality, completeness, mostly because it was made up of 3 + 4, the trinity and the world, the triangle and the square, and so held the secret of the universe. This was why there were 7 sacraments, 7 virtues, 7 deadly sins, etc. Such arithmetico-mystical attitudes to numbers have vanished, apart from various childish jingles and abiding superstitions, which remind us of their disappearance. Perfectly rational people refuse to take room number 13 in a hotel – indeed, some hotels refuse to have a room or floor of that number. And the way we teach children to count blackbirds is revealing:

1 for sorrow
2 for joy
3 for a wedding
4 for a boy
5 for silver
6 for gold
7 for a secret never to be told.

The nursery rhyme, as often, contains far more than it pretends, and the number 7 is representative of some hidden wisdom which helps us to understand the world we live in. There is no necessity to develop further the arithmetico-mystical tradition which inspired our forefathers, from Pythagoras, who said 'everything is number,' right through the whole of the Middle Ages.3 Our present very restricted and univocal interpretation of numbers is not more than three centuries old and is not shared by other cultures. The purpose of these reminders is to sensitise readers to another way of looking at numbers, which is not to be discounted and which will be helpful when approaching our reading of the tarot cards. Such an idiom will align the 4 cardinal virtues, the 4 gospels, the 4 elements and the 4 corners of the earth in a way that is symbolic. So also 7 days, 7 planets, 7 churches, 7 gifts of the Spirit, 7 deadly sins, 7 pillars of Wisdom, 7 petitions in the Lord's prayer, provide the symbol of universality much more effectively to a certain mind-set than a more accurate tally of scientific exactitude. It is a matter of world-view. In certain countries in Africa, for instance, if a woman is asked her age when she is about to get married for the (Western European) purposes of registration, she will reply 21, not because that is her chronological age (which she may not know and may care less about), but because it is the age one gets married at. The mentality which devised the tarot accepted that number was the most exact representation of the unknowable (the secret meanings of the cosmos), and therefore one set about finding evidences of significant numbers throughout the universe.

Such a mind finds instances of the Trinity everywhere. The 'frozen eloquence' of cathedral architecture is basically that of number, in which the very sum of pillars, gates, windows is meaningful.4 The altar steps are 3 or some multiple thereof, the baptismal font is octagonal because 8 is the number of infinity, salvation is on the 8th day.

In alchemy, the symbol of chemical change was the dragon or salamander devouring its tail, thus forming a circle and bearing the mystical motto of 3 words and 7 letters *en tó pan* (meaning: 'all is one' in Greek), which gives, by adding the 3 + 7 of both the words and the letters, the unity of the decad: 10, which signifies completeness, finality, perfection. It is also important to recognise that the dominant medieval attitude towards number was Christian, mostly elaborated from the numerology of Augustine, and that the most extensive and profound employment of these symbolic numbers was made by the Church both for exegetical and liturgical purposes. The medieval church gathered together all the wisdom about numbers from every pagan and pre-Christian source and wedded these to the teachings of the church. Various geometrical shapes assumed a similar significance. The cross, the square, the circle, the pentacle, the pentangle (5-pointed star), had symbolic shape and significance corresponding to numbers. All medieval life, literature and mind-set are symbolic.

In a story called 'The Trump of Death' taken from *The Gesta Romanorum*5, a king puts his brother in a deep pit sitting on a chair which has 4 rotten legs. He hangs a sword over his head and puts 4 men with swords at each point of the compass around him. He then calls for music and food and questions his brother about why he is so miserable. When the reply comes he takes the trouble to explain this 'symbolic' situation. His brother's plight is the same as his own. He, as king, is sitting on a throne that is just as frail and transient as the rotting chair. His body is made up of the 4 elements suspended over the pit of hell. The sword of justice hangs above; in front is

the sword of death; behind is the sword of sin; to his right is the
sword of the Devil; and to his left the sword of disintegration.
Such dramatic charades are the atmospheric symbolism in
which the tarot cards are bathed. And their composition was
emergent from a crucible of Christian symbolism.

The third adjustment we have to make is in terms of
causality. We have to recognise that for about 1500 years, from
Aristotle (383–322 BCE) to Galileo (1564–1642), everyone in
Europe believed they were living in the same world. What you
get is what you see: they had confidence in empirical
perception. The world around us was more or less the way it
appeared to the human mind as delivered to that mind by the
senses. This world was made up of substantial self-contained
bodies. These were made up of four elements: fire, air, water,
earth. Every body had a natural place (geometrically locatable by
Euclidean geometry), which therefore presupposed an absolute
space. Space was the receptacle of all sensible things. These
were all extended in space and contained by a place. There
could be no empty space. Nature abhorred a vacuum. Bodies
were at rest by nature and if moved they were moved by
another. And when moved they sought to return to their
natural place by those inherent qualities of heaviness or
lightness. The most reassuring axiom which we all believed for
over 1500 years was that our solid earth was the stable centre of
a system of concentric spheres to which the heavenly bodies
were attached. These heavenly bodies moved and operated
'necessarily' as opposed to our earth, which was subject to
change. 'Necessary' meant 'what always happens in the same
way': the sun, moon, planets and stars moved by the spheres,
moved as predictably as spheres, operated from successively
different positions and therefore they supplied the earth with a
perpetual and periodic regime of change.

Nowadays we get a great laugh at our ancestors being
taken in by such a naïve explanation, and we throw up our
hands in horror at the way Galileo and his interfering friends
were treated when they began to observe what was actually

happening and to suggest that everyone had got it wrong. However, the scientific method they introduced and the explanations that they offered, and which presided for the next three hundred years, have proved to be myopic and misleading also. How did we arrive at the point of scientific theory where we come to understand the way in which matter interacts in terms of what is known as quantum mechanics? How does this field stand on the shoulders of what is known as classical mechanics? When did we start to apply the language of mathematics to the study of matter? Yeats puts it pithily in one of his 'Fragments':

> Locke sank into a swoon;
> The Garden died;
> God took the spinning-jenny
> Out of his side.

John Locke (1632–1704) was the philosopher responsible in great part for empiricism. Empirical science related things not to our senses but to each other. Observation gave way to measurement. Measurement related things to each other. Like William Blake (1757–1827), Yeats saw Descartes, Locke and Newton as materialists 'who took away the world and gave us its excrement instead'. These were the fathers of those three centuries of sleep which substituted sterile abstractions for real contact with the world. 'It is customary to praise English empirical genius, English sense of reality... [W]ho does not serve these abstractions? Without them corporate life would be impossible... And of all these the most comprehensive, the most useful, was invented by Locke when he separated the primary and secondary qualities; and from that day to this the conception of a physical world without colour, sound, taste, tangibility, ... has remained the assumption of science, the groundwork of every text-book. It worked, and the mechanical inventions of the next age, its symbols that seemed its confirmation, worked even better.'[6] Classical mechanics arose from the banishment of consciousness from our conception of the physical universe. Scientists looked for principles and laws which would be the same for all observers because they were outside the range of observational activity. Mathematical expression of such physical principles and laws would be invariant. Mechanics studies the relations of masses not to our senses but to one another. Physics studies the relations of types of energy, not to our senses but to one another.

The univocal view of number and *The Mathematical Principles of Natural Philosophy* written by Isaac Newton in 1687, narrowed even further our view of the world and our way of explaining it. As A. N. Whitehead puts it: 'The seventeenth century produced a scheme of scientific thought framed by mathematicians for the use of mathematicians.'[7] Contemporary physics would have been satisfied if it could find a formula that would account for the complete chain of mechanical causation in the universe.

The end of the nineteenth century marked the peak of classical physics. Scientists felt they had achieved a sound body of work and that progress would mean theoretical advancement on what had already been accomplished over the last three centuries. Newton and Lagrange reigned supreme over the world of particles. This theory implied that the only kind of body found in the universe was made up of particles and that each particle occupied a point in space. Maxwell and Lorenz ruled the world of waves. Both these worlds were separate and complete. A new way of thinking emerged with quantum mechanics, which involved a theory of matter and of the mechanical action between particles, which would introduce us to wave mechanics as opposed to a matrix mechanics.

In the 1960s David Bohm (1917–1992) began to take a closer look at the notion of what we refer to as order. One day he saw on television two concentric glass cylinders with the space between them being filled with glycerin, a sticky, glutinous fluid. A drop of ink in the fluid becomes extended into a thread so thin it eventually disappears, if viewed through the outer cylinder. This means that the ink particles have been 'enfolded' into the glycerin. But if the cylinder is turned in the opposite direction, the thin thread reappears and turns back into a drop; which means that this drop has been 'unfolded' all over again. This led Bohm to understand that the ink diffused through the glycerin was not in a state of 'disorder', but rather a hidden, or non-manifest, order. This illustrated his revolutionary view that everything in the world makes up a continuum. Even though everything looks separate to us, they are all a seamless extention of each other. This underlying substrate is what he calls the 'implicate' order; the 'explicate' order is how they appear to us as separate and discrete parts, as the different things that surround each one of us. He illustrates this idea by using a flowing stream:

> On this stream, one may see an ever-changing pattern of vortices, ripples, waves, splashes, etc., which evidently have no independent existence as such. Rather, they are abstracted from the flowing movement, arising and vanishing in the total process of the flow. Such transitory subsistence as may be possessed by these abstracted forms implies only a relative independence or autonomy of behaviour, rather than absolutely independent existence as ultimate substances.[8]

Another way of illustrating the 'implicate' order is the hologram. To make a hologram, a laser light is split into two beams, one of which is reflected off an object onto a photographic plate, where it interferes with the second beam. The complex swirls of the interference pattern recorded on the photographic plate appear meaningless and disordered to the naked eye. But like the ink drop dispersed in the glycerin, the pattern possesses a hidden or enfolded order, for when illuminated with laser light it produces a three-dimensional image of the original object, which can be viewed from any angle. A remarkable feature of a hologram is that if a holographic film is cut into pieces, each piece produces an image of the whole object, though the smaller the piece the hazier the image. Clearly the form and structure of the entire object are encoded within each region of the photographic record.

Bohm suggests that the whole universe can be thought of as a kind of giant, flowing hologram, or holomovement, in which a total order is contained, in some implicit sense, in each region of space and time. Bohm sees life and consciousness as enfolded deep in the generative order and therefore present in varying degrees of unfoldment in all matter, including supposedly 'inanimate' matter such as electrons or plasmas. He suggests that there is a 'protointelligence' in matter, so that new evolutionary developments do not emerge in a random fashion but creatively as relatively integrated wholes from implicate levels of reality.

Everybody has seen an image of enfoldment, he suggests: You fold up a sheet of paper, turn it into a small packet, make cuts in it, and then unfold it into a pattern. The parts that were close in the cuts unfold to be far away. This is like what happens in a hologram. Enfoldment is really very common in our experience. Another revolutionary thought is that information, which is basically a pattern of energy, is stored at some paraphysical level, and that we can access this information, or exchange information with other minds, if the necessary conditions of 'sympathetic resonance' exist. This would correspond to the communication between Yeats and his wife, to certain telepathic communications, and to premonitions of one kind or another.

C. G. Jung believed that traditional notions of causality were incapable of explaining some of the more improbable forms of coincidence. Where it is plain, felt Jung, that no causal connection can be demonstrated between two events, but where a meaningful relationship nevertheless exists between them, a wholly different type of principle is likely to be operating. Jung called this principle 'synchronicity'.

In *The Structure and Dynamics of the Psyche*, Jung describes how, during his research into the phenomenon of the collective unconscious, he began to observe coincidences that were connected in such a meaningful way that their occurrence seemed to defy the calculations of probability. He provided numerous examples taken from his own case studies:

> A young woman I was treating had, at a critical moment, a dream in which she was given a golden scarab. While she was telling me this dream I sat with my back to the closed window. Suddenly I heard a noise behind me, like a gentle tapping. I turned round and saw a flying insect knocking against the window-pane from outside. I opened the window and caught the creature in the air as it flew in. It was the nearest analogy to the golden scarab that one finds in our latitudes, a scarabaeid beetle, the common rose-chafer (*Cetoaia urata*) which contrary to its usual habits had evidently felt an urge to get into a dark room at this particular moment. I must admit that nothing like it ever happened to me before or since, and that the dream of the patient has remained unique in my experience.[9]

In his paper 'Synchronicity: an A-causal connecting principle', he defines this term as

> ... the parallelism of time and meaning between psychic and psychophysical events, which scientific knowledge so far has been unable to reduce to a common principle. The term explains nothing, it simply formulates the occurrence of meaningful coincidences which, in themselves, are chance happenings, but are so improbable that we must assume them to be based on some kind of principle, or on some property of the empirical world. No reciprocal causal connection can be shown to obtain between parallel events, which is just what gives them their chance character. The only recognizable and demonstrable link between them is a common meaning, or equivalence.[10]

I am not saying either that I understand all these proposals about the world we live in, about time and space, what I am saying is that the very simplified and cosy versions of these, which were commonplace and satisfying to our ancestors, are now obsolete. A much more subtle and complicated vision of the universe is being forced upon us.

The tarot cards present us with a way of approaching the future which is comprehensive and inventive enough to cater for whatever explanation may emerge. I go further than this and with Doris Lessing affirm the possibility that the causality of chance is the means whereby God can enter our universe while remaining anonymous. God uses coincidence to nudge us in the direction of wholeness, which is sometimes too difficult or intricate for us to contemplate without some prompting. Such unusual occurrences have been recorded by many inventors, explorers, artists. It is as if when on the brink of some great breakthrough, nature conspires with those who have exercised themselves conscientiously on behalf of that evolutionary appetite which leads us towards a better future for humankind to show us the way. Things turn up, people cross our paths, dates and incidents coincide to reveal a pattern which, in turn, shows us the path we took before. When you've done everything in your power and you still can't get the thing to click, the Gods throw down fire. Or, less dramatically, the world lights up some hidden clue, and ordinary things reveal themselves as secret signs. Such is the symbolic infrastructure of the universe.

The problem with our inherited world is not the hierarchy of different symbolic systems that are available to us to interpret the spectrum of experience which spans the radar screen of human consciousness, it is, rather, the dearth of such systems when it comes to neglected areas, especially those which are unconscious. We have only to think of the language of emotion to find an area where education and trained sensibility are in short supply. Each person is left to fend for themselves in one of the most poignant and inescapable areas of our experience. And yet it seems obvious that each of us should be given at least the rudiments of one of the most elusive and important symbolic systems if we are even to begin to understand human relationships. This would require tapping into a wavelength and a communications system other than the cerebral, reaching what has been called the 'sympathetic system' as opposed to the cerebro-spinal one which covers the three Rs of traditional education.

However, the specific interest of this book is to provide some help in the even more subtle and neglected area of training ourselves to deal with the unconscious. There are ways and means of heightening our awareness of this huge but hidden area of our lives. There is a language of symbols that can help us to grapple with the unconscious. The middle ages were fluent in such dialect. The world was a multi-layered tableau of symbols. As above, so below; as in the foreground so in the background: there was a correspondence between everything in heaven and on earth and the medieval mind was attuned to the connections that should and could be made. Hidden signs and symbols connected the phenomenal universe. These revealed themselves in similar qualities and associations, whether audible or visible: colour and shape, volume and weight, texture and movement, these could be compared and aligned just as sounds, if similar, could unveil a code of correspondence.

The major arcana of the tarot present an array of faces jumping out of the ocean of the unconscious. They are dummies for us to clothe with our own symbolism; targets through which to shoot our particular spleen; transparencies to slot into our psychological projectors; decoys which can help us to hook and unravel the otherwise invisible threads of our unconscious side of the tapestry of life. The fact that they are cards allows us to deal them at random and allows the play of coincidence, which both undermines our own fetishistic flair for order and allows the possibility of ingenious intervention from without. This spread of colourful phantasmagoria is a kinetic icon of whatever is deepest in ourselves, and the deepest layer of that reality is our search for God. 'Called or uncalled, God will be there.'[11]

CHAPTER FIVE

A CHRISTIAN READING OF THE TAROT?

The Western world of the twenty-first century is one where religion seems to have been discredited. And yet most of us long for some access to the spiritual. At many moments of our lives we know that this dimension is what we need, but we don't have keys to unlock these doors. Churches and institutions have betrayed our trust. Even if the inner core remains unblemished, so much is tarnished and corrupt on the outside that we find it sordid and compromising to use as a way through. We look for something evocative, something tangible, something available to us in our own homes, on train journeys, in moments that take us unawares.

What we need is a medium, a sacrament: something already existing in this world of ours which can act as a window to another world, a world beyond the one we inhabit as living bodies whose only sustenance is sensual and corporeal. The truth is that anything in this world of ours can act as such a God bearer. Most things have done so for religiously sensitive people in the past. A bush, a river, a mountain, a valley, a cave, a song, a sound, a book, a picture, a voice, an animal, a bird, a word, water, oil, vinegar, bread and wine, all have been used as instruments of God's real presence in our world. However, some very special instruments have been refined over the centuries and are recognised as transparent icons of this mysterious presence in our lives.

The strange but important truth is that this presence can never be immediately transparent, uncomplicatedly available. God has to be God and we have to be ourselves, and never the twain shall meet in the same time-space dimension, because this very dimension had to be invented so that we could stand on our own two feet without being reabsorbed into God. So this barrier is our only safeguard as human beings. And it means in turn that we cannot know God directly either: there is, there has to be, a secret wisdom, which subverts our natural capacity to know, which is constitutionally incapable of direct beatific vision. We have to know in the way we were made, in the way that we are. This is because we were born with a mind and there is nothing we can do about it. The mind came with the body, they go as a set. And this mind-set requires that if we want to 'know' God, we have to learn and develop a secret wisdom that goes against the grain of natural wisdom. This secret wisdom is about the presence of God in our world, which cannot be other than secret. If it were manifest it would be so obvious that there would be no freedom on our part to know or love God. Our freedom demands that any knowledge of the God who made us must be hidden in the world God made. Like an expert thief, God had to steal himself away without leaving any obvious clues behind which would identify the world as his manufacture.

So, the reason why knowledge of God is hidden is because our minds are otherwise focused, our interest is elsewhere, and our education trains us to overlook it. We are fashioned like the detectives in that story by Edgar Allen Poe about the stolen letter. We search the house and every room, in all the places we have learnt to search for hidden items: under the carpet, inside the panels of drawers, behind the skirting of the floor boards, behind picture frames, unscrewing legs of chairs to examine spaces between these, tapping on walls to locate hollow crevices, when all the time the letter escaped our notice in a letter rack on the mantelpiece. The presence of God in our world is so obvious that we fail to notice it, just as we completely ignore the watches on our wrists, don't even know we have one on, until we need it to tell us a certain kind of time. The truth is that we are too clever by half to recognise the obvious. Our minds are oblivious to it, as they are to the glasses on our noses or the contact lenses in our eyes which allow some of us to see.

Our conscious minds are otherwise occupied. However, there is that vast ocean of the unconscious where the presence of God can lurk without ever being detected. Once again, the difficulty is accessing this undiscovered continent. At the end of the nineteenth and the beginning of the twentieth centuries people in Europe became aware of this wider, deeper area of consciousness. Freud and Jung were pioneers in the area of psychotherapy, by which 'patients' of theirs could get in touch with their unconscious by almost scientific means. Artists who were their contemporaries shunned their rather crude approach and explored their own speciality of art work as a way through. Many people became obsessed by the possibility of contacting the spirits of the dead. This is perfectly understandable when one situates the preoccupation in the unimagined horror of the First World War. *The Times*, of London, for instance, carried daily at least two pages of columns of names of deceased soldiers. Both the unprecedented number of the slaughtered and the communication of this horror by radio and newspaper made a whole generation aware of the shortness, flimsiness, abruptness of life on earth. There had to be something more, something beyond. People who claimed to be in contact with this world, where the recent dead had gone without a word, were sought out and lionised by the desperate bereaved.

Mediums and occultists who used ouija boards, tarot cards, table-tapping sessions, were all the rage in a certain leisured society. All of these were seeking access to a hidden wisdom which was somewhere out there. Those who claimed to be professionally equipped to understand both the cause and the results of such questing seemed to suggest that there was nothing 'out there', and anything that appeared to come from such a neverneverland came from the unconscious. Many early psychotherapists were atheists, and they included all so-called communication with God in this category of ourselves talking

to ourselves unconsciously. C. G. Jung is a case in point. Many
have accused him of saying that God was an invention of our
unconscious. So important has Jung been in offering us access,
maps and imaginative ways of filtering this strange underworld
into our workaday lives that it is important to examine what he
actually does say. In his 'Answer to Job' Jung says the following
about psychology and religion in the West:

> If the individuation process is made conscious,
> consciousness must confront the unconscious and a
> balance between the opposites must be found. As this is not
> possible through logic, one is dependent on symbols which
> make the irrational union of opposites possible. They are
> produced spontaneously by the unconscious and are
> amplified by the conscious mind. The central symbols of
> this process describe the self, which is man's totality,
> consisting on the one hand of that which is conscious to
> him, and on the other hand of the contents of the
> unconscious... This is only a very summary sketch of the
> process, but it can be observed at any time in modern man,
> or one can read about it in the documents of Hermetic
> philosophy from the Middle Ages. The parallelism between
> the symbols is astonishing to anyone who knows both the
> psychology of the unconscious and alchemy. The difference
> between the 'natural' individuation process, which runs its
> course unconsciously, and the one which is consciously
> realised, is tremendous. In the first case consciousness
> nowhere intervenes; the end remains as dark as the
> beginning. In the second case so much darkness comes to
> light that the personality is permeated with light, and
> consciousness necessarily gains in scope and insight... It is
> only through the psyche that we can establish that God acts
> upon us, but we are unable to distinguish whether these
> actions emanate from God or from the unconscious. We
> cannot tell whether God and the unconscious are two
> different entities. Both are border-line concepts for

transcendental contents. But empirically it can be established, with a sufficient degree of probability, that there is in the unconscious an archetype of wholeness which manifests itself spontaneously in dreams etc., and a tendency, independent of the conscious will, to relate other archetypes to this centre. Consequently, it does not seem improbable that the archetype of wholeness occupies as such a central position which approximates it to the God-image. The similarity is further borne out by the peculiar fact that the archetype produces a symbolism which has always characterised and expressed the Deity. These facts make possible a certain qualification of our above thesis concerning the indistinguishableness of God and the unconscious. Strictly speaking, the God-image does not coincide with the unconscious as such, but with a special content of it, namely the archetype of the self. It is this archetype from which we can no longer distinguish the God-image empirically. We can arbitrarily postulate a difference between these two entities, but that does not help us at all... Only that which acts upon me do I recognise as real and actual. But that which has no effect upon me might as well not exist. The religious need longs for wholeness, and therefore lays hold of the images of wholeness offered by the unconscious, which, independently of the conscious mind, rise up from the depths of our psychic nature.[1]

The unconscious harbours a blueprint for our wholeness, it contains the map of how we should and could reach completion. We cannot be sure that this blueprint comes from God, according to Jung; we have no way of distinguishing in this vast ocean of possibility what comes from ourselves and what comes from outside ourselves. But one thing is sure, each one of us does hold within this deep instinctual space an intuition about ourselves, about which direction we should be taking and what could lead to our own fulfilment. We can live our lives without any contact between ourselves and this unconscious, and this means that we simply ride the waves of life like a cowboy trying to stay aboard a bucking bronco. We are thrown around and smashed into shape without any cooperation on our part, without any notion about what is going on or why it might be happening to us.

On the other hand, if we do try to make this hidden intuition conscious and if we work conscientiously with the hints that our unconscious provides, prompting us towards whatever actions are necessary for our salvation, then we become cooperative riders in the chariot of life. And this combination makes for human progress of a kind that becomes lined into the contours of our faces and knitted into the structure of our bones. It is a human success story for those who practise it, more effective than any bestselling guide to greatness, self-improvement therapy, or handbook for wholeness. The secret of who we really are is inscribed within.

Connecting the unconscious to the conscious is done by working symbolically. Jung states that such work hinges upon an archetypal theology which is indistinguishable from human rehabilitation. In the unconscious there are no boundary limitations, no frontiers on the map which can allow us to determine consciously where we end and where God begins, where the promptings that emerge are self-elicited or God-given. But there is no other channel for connecting us with what is not us.

This is a very far cry from saying that God does not exist, that God is our own invention, that God is a name for our own image of perfection, the title of our human development programme. Such are the conclusions which many have drawn from reading these texts of Jung, and such texts provide the bases for condemnation of him as an atheist and of his theories as hedonist and selfish vindication of our baser instincts.

Since the world began there has always been a hidden wisdom, a secret knowledge handed on from one generation to the next, mostly by rituals or ceremonies because it was not possible to carry such knowledge in formulae or books. It was the secret knowledge about the presence of God and about God's care for us. Such things are so delicate and refined that they can only be communicated to those we can trust enough. Those in possession of such knowledge are persecuted by others who fear them, despise them, mistrust them or are jealous of them. For many years and in many countries the secret knowledge about God's coming down to earth and dwelling with human beings was scandalous to some, folly to others, a dangerous threat to those who did not believe in God or who believed in other very different kinds of God.

There were at least two people who were aware of this secret knowledge and who tried to create an artistic medium which could make it available to the rest of humankind. These were the apostles of Jesus Christ, John and Paul. Those who have ears to hear with could and can avail of the wisdom they provided. Many others had tried, have tried, before and after these two, to describe this wisdom in different ways. Nearly every tribe on the planet has had individuals in its ranks who became aware of this secret knowledge, in however hazy a way, and tried to lay hands on it, so that they in turn could hand it on to their children. Some used hieroglyphs, others used alphabets, others used rituals, others used cults. The word used for such 'handing on' of the secret knowledge is a Latin word 'tradition', which in its original form could mean 'to betray' as easily as it meant to hand on. Christ was 'handed over' by Judas in the Garden of Gethsemane with the same word as his Gospel was 'handed down' by his beloved disciple. So there is a very thin line between 'saying it as it is' and 'betraying it as it is'.

It is also true that at the deepest level of the unconscious in humanity every kind of expression is imbued with, is energised by, this ever-active hidden wisdom which pervades our world. Even such innocent utterings as fairy tales and nursery rhymes contain within them a depth of wisdom that those who enunciated them were quite unaware of. And yet the unconscious used these mantras and cries to smuggle into our world a truth that was deeper and more important for us than the nonchalant riddles we were rhyming.

When both the hidden wisdom and the inspired writer are at their most conscious and at the highest register of communication, the result is a sacred text with layer upon layer of hidden meaning clinging like phosphorescence to the writer's weave. The writings of St John the Evangelist, for instance, are the most mystical and esoteric of all the Christian scriptures. St John himself was aware that the mystery, the secret knowledge, he was trying to impart through his faltering words, could never be contained in writing of any kind. If everything were to be written down, he acknowledged, the whole world could not contain the books that would have to be written. However, the texts which he did write are acknowledged by all to be some of the most sacred ever elaborated. This also makes them difficult to understand, polyvalent in terms of meaning, open to myriad misinterpretation. It is not difficult to understand why they were very quickly appropriated by various churches and translated into dogmatic creeds, moral precepts and spiritual formulae, easily imparted, understood and digested by the obedient followers of whichever denomination.

The so-called mystery religions and gnostic cults which attempted to articulate such wisdom in more mystical and veiled ways were violently opposed and suppressed throughout the history of the churches. The only accounts we have of them must be gleaned from documents surviving from those who only described them to condemn them outright. In fact, the only source of such 'doctrines' must have been compiled by some Byzantine scholars in the second or third centuries, and these texts were lost to Western Europe. They only became known after their discovery by an Italian monk around 1460 and their later translation by Marsilio Ficini at the request of Cosimo de Medici. This *Corpus Hermeticum* became a somewhat sanitised Reader's Digest of occult knowledge and magical practice. However, there must have been many more and many other variations of these attempts to plumb the length and the breadth, the height and the depth of the mysteries of religion. Such traditions lived on among individuals and tiny sects, mostly condemned as heretical.

In such an atmosphere it is no wonder that such so-called Hermetic literature and rituals were secret in every manifestation; nor is it surprising that the tarot cards came to be associated with such knowledge. Their dissemination occurred at the same time as the discovery of the *Corpus Hermeticum*, which excited the readers in Europe at the dawn of the Renaissance. It was even suggested that the Cathars and Albigensians who were situated in Provence, receiving the second of these names from the town of Albi, had used the Tarot of Marseilles, which is nearby, as a way of preserving their version of Christianity before they were ruthlessly obliterated.

Eliphas Lévi (1810–1875), once a Roman Catholic priest, must be credited with being the first person both to make a comprehensive synthesis of all that is known about Western Hermeticism and for integrating the tarot cards into this system. And it is true that the cards are symbolic and can therefore be used for many purposes, including that of meditating on the Christian mystery, since the imagery and symbolism they contain are essentially Christian. However, the cards themselves are no more than a vehicle.

A medium, any medium, and its plural 'media', 'the Media', as we have become all too familiar with it today, is as powerful, as moral and as responsible as whatever or whoever is using it. In itself it is neutral. It is a go-between, an intermediary, as insignificant as the servant in great houses of the past who was known deprecatingly as a 'tweeny', the one who moved 'between' the upstairs and the downstairs. The tarot is just such a 'tweeny', moving mercurially, hermetically, between the upstairs of the mind and the downstairs of the unconscious.

We should be aware of this today: perhaps the most powerful medium that has ever been put at our disposal is the internet. It puts us in touch with every corner of the globe and potentially with every person on the planet. Everyone is aware of its benefits; just as most of us are aware of the crimes which are committed every minute through its mediumship and which could never have been perpetrated to this extent without it. So, do we condemn it as evil because evil people can use it for their purposes? Many might say: yes. But it doesn't really matter what they say, because the internet is here to stay. Its positive effect on the quality of our lives outweighs the negative spin-offs that abuse of its all-pervading and prolific services inevitably entail. So aware are we of the universality and positivity of its overall effect that we want to introduce everybody to its benefits and shrink from excluding anyone, even when they declare themselves to be hostile or allergic.

That is also why I want to introduce you to the tarot. It is one of the simplest and most attractive ways of making contact with a world beyond the one we so naturally inhabit. It can offer an easy way to meditate. It is a beautiful and attainable work of art: a portable art gallery, a pocket painting course. It is an introduction to art for the colour-blind. It can be for many people who find art inaccessible an alternative way of thinking artistically. And it could be for most a port-hole to the underworld.

For three centuries it has been hijacked by occultists and cartomancers, to the extent that it has got a bad name. People flee from it. I have heard it called 'the devil's pack'. It has become something of a scapegoat. And yet, before this happened, it was used in a perfectly harmless context and developed within a tradition of Christian symbolism. That it is monopolised by profiteers and fortune tellers, barred by scaremongerers and alarmists, forbidden by authorities in both state and church, is understandable. The cards can be a source of individual integration and personal autonomy unwelcome to those who seek control over others. They do provide access to areas of ourselves which are dangerous for the weak-minded and pusillanimous, and they can become a source of imbalance and even breakdown if handled incautiously.[2] In the evolutionary history of Western humanity it was only in the twentieth century of our so-called civilisation that unlimited and universal access to the unconscious was offered through the mediumship of psychoanalysis. Before that time only artists and prophets of one kind or another had appropriated the key.

What I am trying to offer here is an introduction to an artistic tool, like a chisel or a paintbrush, even a personal computer, which gives access to much more than itself, as a window, a password, a key. Playing with the tarot is an exercise of the imagination. Imagination is given very little attention or scope in our present system of education, or, indeed, in the way most of us run our lives. Such neglect ensures that a powerful, limitless, creative area of ourselves remains dormant, unused, untapped.

And, whatever about other possibilities opened for us by the tarot, it is important, even necessary, for us to connect with the unconscious. How we do so is a matter of temperament or taste. It can be through dreams or through art or through whatever kind of psychoanalysis. The way is less important than the goal. And if the twentieth century has taught us anything, it is that such connection is no longer an optional extra. It is a sociological and hygienic obligation.

As well as the psychological or sociological level, there is another way of reading them, which is the most fundamental aspect of this book. Just as we project onto people the archetypes that lie in the depths of our unconscious, so we project onto God the stereotypes that have accumulated in the attic or the basement over the centuries in this regard. And yet, as in the world of dreams, if we examine them in depth and in detail, we can discover a great deal of truth hidden in the art of these icons from the unconscious. And so, in the reading of each of these cards in turn, we will be able to detect a teaching that can help us both to understand and to direct our spiritual lives.

The cards were developed in a pan-Christian society where symbolism and thought-patterns were essentially

Christian, and they have been used over the intervening centuries by theologians and spiritual writers to provide a way of meditating upon the deepest mysteries of the Christian message. The book which has provided me with inspiration for much of what is written here about the tarot was composed by an anonymous author who had his work published after his death in 1973. He was born in Russia in 1900, became a disciple of Rudolph Steiner before converting to Catholicism. His major work, called *Meditations on the Tarot, A Journey into Christian Hermeticism*, was originally written in French and was completed in 1967. The German translation, which appeared in 1983, contained a preface by one of the great Roman Catholic theologians of the twentieth century, Hans Urs Von Balthasar.[3]

In this introduction 'to what must be for most readers a somewhat strange if not alien, but at the same time very enriching book', Von Balthasar says:

> What we have before us here is so thought-provoking that no one could remain indifferent to it. A praying and thinking Christian presents us here, with compelling sincerity, the symbolism of Christian Hermeticism, arranging this in order – Mysticism, Gnosis and Magic – and seeking to integrate these within the all-encompassing umbrella of Catholic mystery wisdom, meditatively drawing upon the Jewish Cabbala, the elements of wisdom in alchemy and astrology, and the symbolism of the so-called 'great arcana' of the 22 Tarot cards.

Von Balthasar shows that similar attempts have been made in the philosophical and theological history of the Catholic Church. Many of the fathers of the Church believed that even pagan fantasy about the mythological world contained veiled hints that prefigured and found fulfilment in Jesus Christ as the all-encompassing Logos. Origen in particular perfected this line of thought: Christ could integrate and explain all wisdom of the pagans and of the Old Testament, as well as 'the wisdom of the princes of this world' (I Cor. 2:6). In Origen's case such wisdom would include the so-called secret philosophy of the Egyptians, the hermetic writings allegedly stemming through 'Hermes Trismegistos' from the Egyptian God Thoth, 'the astrology of the Chaldeans and the Indians, the multi-faceted teachings of the Greeks on the Divine. Origen believed that these worldly wisdoms were not being communicated to humankind to hurt or do damage, but as preparation for the Gospel. Von Balthasar suggests that a great number of Fathers of the Church had found an honourable place for Hermes Trismegistos as bearer of the wisdom of the heathen prophets. Hermetic literature was circulated widely during the early and higher Middle Ages; later, Hermes was celebrated as a contemporary of Moses and as ancestral source of Greek wisdom. (Von Balthasar quotes the imposing portrait of Hermes embedded in the floor of the cathedral in Sienna.) The theology of Von Balthasar teaches that if poets, artists and theologians were able to salvage in such sources and in other pagan teachers of wisdom, respectfully and enthusiastically, scattered rays of divine light, and follow these back to their point of incandescence in Jesus Christ, other similar exercises in rehabilitation and retrieval are not only possible but essential. He finds this even more importantly in terms of the Jewish Cabbala, whose secret oral tradition is meant to date back to the time of Moses:

> The important thing is that this incursion into pagan and Jewish hermetic knowledge took place in the spirit of humanism which hoped to revivify an ossified Christian theology by injecting into it these scattered rays of revelation from elsewhere. These humanists never doubted for a moment that they could integrate any and all disparate knowledge into genuine Christian belief.

Von Balthasar is clear that the anonymous author of this book on the tarot for which he is writing a preface, has given adequate assurance on this point. 'Of particular interest', he claims, 'is the fact that these meditations spring from the old symbolic pictures of the Tarot. Naturally the author is aware of the magical divination for which these cards can be used. However he does not feel in any way constrained from using the polyvalent word 'magic'. He is not interested, through these meditations, in joining any divinatory card game. What is significant for him are the pictures or ideas contained in the cards, whether as individual symbols or as a constellation of inter-related symbolic systems. Since he quotes Jung quite often, it would be possible, with caution, to call these archetypes. However, we should guard against interpreting them merely as inner psychological data of the collective unconscious, which, indeed, Jung himself categorically refuses to do. They can equally be understood as principles of the objective cosmos and in such capacity enter the domain of what the Bible refers to as 'principalities and powers'. Finally, Von Balthasar gives a moving verdict on this book of meditations which, it is my hope, could also be applied to my own:

He steeps himself with loving seriousness in the symbols before him. They inspire him and he allows himself to give free vent to his imagination scanning the depths of the world and of the soul. Whenever the memory of something known or read previously occurs to him through his meditation, he includes it. The exigency of his thought lies less in detail – frequently the streams of thought cross into one another – as in the abiding conviction that everything hangs together in the depths, and that each thing points analogically to every other thing. Even the most abstruse individual insights are held magnetically in thrall to an overarching and unifying power by which they are subjugated and placed in their order. Such thraldom, for him, is very precisely not that vulgar magical need to control of the person who tries to dominate through cleverness, knowledge or the powers of this world. It is sometimes quite other than this: something that can only be called 'the magic of grace', whose influence stems from the central mysteries of the Catholic faith.

Von Balthasar compares this book of meditation with

the thriving trade of the gutter press and other trashy literature, peddling cheap horoscopes which are ill adapted to individual need, replacing faith by farfetched superstition. And all this in areas where expert training, serious moral responsibility, and even more than either of these, a certain sixth sense, a feeling for the limits of what can be communicated, a respectful reticence in face of the distinct religious journey of every individual, should be absolute requirements.

On the contrary, he says,

the work we have before us rises far above such abuses. In its design it is a 'meditation' which refuses to provide any concrete indications of how, under the guidance of Christian wisdom, the 'occult sciences' can be applied in practice. Perhaps such esoteric instruction is beyond the competence of this author. His only concern is to present an analogy showing how all levels of wordly theoretical and practical knowledge tend towards the incarnation of the divine logos as the original prototype and remain anchored to this reality, as if suspended on a chain.

I emphasise two most important principles issuing from this precise and subtle critique from one of the foremost Catholic theologians of the twentieth century: the first is that since the appearance of the Logos incarnate on earth, all secret wisdom has been revealed and any wisdom that genuinely searches for the truth is eventually compatible with the comprehensive unfolding of this all-embracing Truth. The corollary is that every manifestation of secret wisdom is potentially a tributary to that ocean of truth. Heresy is the Greek word for being too selective, for cutting off a part, forming a sect, when only the truth, the whole truth and nothing but the truth should be our goal. *Meditations on the Tarot, A Journey into Christian Hermeticism* is a deep and often difficult study of over 650 pages. It has been a major source for the commentary on the 22 cards which follows. To reduce footnotes and facilitate reference I shall refer to it as MT in the text and give the appropriate page numbers.[4]

The second book which has been a source for many of the insights which I record as I present each of the 22 cards of the major arcana of the tarot is by Sallie Nichols, a woman who studied at the Jung Institute in Zurich while C. G. Jung was himself alive and active there. It is called *Jung and Tarot, An Archetypal Journey.*[5] I will refer to this book as SN in the text. It complements the approach of the first-mentioned by offering several interpretations in the light of Jungian psychology. But it also gives the point of view of a woman, which is so germane to my own that it emphasises the fundamental human reality we are dealing with here, both male and female. With these two companions I hope to present a traditional and compelling interpretation of the tarot as psychological aid and spiritual guide. What is being offered in these pages is not original. It is a tradition, a wisdom handed down over many centuries and contained in the arcana of the tarot in symbolic form. The purpose of this book is to make that wisdom available to readers of this twenty-first century in as accessible a form as possible.

And so to the cards themselves. I present each card as it appears in the Marseilles deck and with a meditation which is rooted in the artistic composition and symbolic representation of each one, and the suggestive order in which they appear. These meditations are a kind of thought which is visual, symbolic and numerate in a way quite different from the literacy, numeracy and logic most of us have been taught. It attempts to introduce the reader to another kind of wisdom, which involves, if you like, the widening and thickening of our normal vision. The way of entry to the cards is through my own personal meditations. This, needless to say, is not intended to be either normative or definitive. Once initiated, it is hoped that each reader will shuffle and deal the symbols and the meditations these evoke in whatever way the Spirit inspires. My own thoughts on each card are not original. They have been sifted from many sources too numerous to mention. They have, however, become my own from many hours of using and meditating the major arcana of the tarot, which are illustrated here before each meditation. Because these meditations are meant to be useful rather than academic, I have kept footnotes to a minimum.

I am not dealing the full pack of cards in this book. I am using only the major arcana as a focus for meditation. These number 22 in all. There is a certain amount of argument about the order and the numbering of these, mostly connected with attempts to align the cards with either alphabetical or zodiacal principles.[6] The number and order in this book is as follows:

Zero   The Fool
I   The Magician
II   The High Priestess
III   The Empress
IIII   The Emperor
V   The Pope
VI   The Lover
VII   The Chariot
VIII   Justice
VIIII   The Hermit
X   The Wheel of Fortune
XI   Strength / Force

XII	The Hanged Man
XIII	Death
XIIII	Temperance
XV	The Devil
XVI	The Tower
XVII	The Star
XVIII	The Moon
XVIIII	The Sun
XX	The Judgement
XXI	The World

In the Marseilles deck, the fool has no number. I follow the tradition which makes him, or her, since there is certainly gender balance in this area, equivalent to zero.

I take the fool to be the tiny zero which is each one of us starting our spiritual journey in the world. The path we tread with this fool, who can appear at any moment in any guise as part of any number on our way, is towards the greater circle of the whole world, which is the last card of the major arcana, card number 21. This card presents itself as a capital O. The complete spread leads us from the lowest common denominator of subjectivity to the highest common factor of objectivity – the subjective world of experience and memory pitted against the objective world of reality and fact. We zig-zag in this presentation of the journey through four groups of five cards. The first five represent the spiritual world, which is both spiritual and psychological, remaining as it does, as they do, mostly in the realm of the unconscious. Our conscious life begins with falling in love. We awake from life as part of the pack with card number 6. We journey on towards maturation until we reach the pinnacle of personal wisdom in card number 9. After this card we are attached to that other circle, which is between the zero of the fool and the higher case nought of the whole world: namely the wheel of fortune. This spins us around to the more objective journey of the last two groups of five. These require the humility of the hanged man, the strength to walk on the real earth (humus), which is the planet impregnated by the sun, the moon and the stars, and not the one cut off from these by a tower of Babel constructed by human hands with the precise purpose of depriving all these of their influence, their connection and their meaning. There is a judgement which is objective and it is the last card in this arrangement of the pack. But I anticipate myself confusingly. Let us begin the journey, taking each step with the particular card designed to be our guide on the way.

PART II
THE MAJOR ARCANA

LE · MAT

THE FOOL

The concept of zero was unknown in the ancient world. The concrete minds of the Greeks could not conceive the void as a number, let alone dignify it with a symbol. How could nothing have a number? The Arabs introduced the world of nothingness. Before this we never thought of quantifying non-existence. We are nothing, and had better begin by examining that reality.

In the history of culture the discovery of zero was one of the great achievements of the human race. Zero tolerance did not appear in Europe until the twelfth century. It is not yet 1,000 years since we discovered that nothing really matters. And the three zeros above, which allow us to picture those thousand years, were some of the most revolutionary insights the world has known.

The discovery of this apparent 'nothing' created the decimal system, the way we stack the cards in tens. The decisive advantage of the Arabic over the Roman decimal system is its positional value. Instead of introducing new symbols at different stages (X for 10 and L for 50), as the Latins did, the Arabs added a 1 to the digit farthest to the left and began a new column each time they had used up the 10.

Until the principle of position was discovered by an unknown Hindu of the first century CE, no further progress in arithmetic was possible. The principle of position means giving the numeral a value that depends not only on the number of the natural sequence it represents, but also on the position it occupies with respect to the other symbols of the group. Thus the same digit 2 has different meanings in these three numbers:

162, 825, 219

where the digit in the third row of the three-numbered sequence is two, in the second row is twenty, whereas at the front it becomes two hundred. Those of us who are numerate perform this exercise without a thought. But the invention of this positional adaptation was a work of genius. It allowed us to move towards this twenty-first century with a speed and dexterity without which we would now be living in a very different world.

All of this seems so simple to us today. However, the one discovery that made this whole system workable was the invention of a sign that told us that even if one of those columns was empty, it still represented not so much 'some thing' as 'no thing'. No progress in numbering was possible until a symbol was invented for an empty class, a symbol for nothing, our modern zero. It was essential to have a way of representing the gaps symbolically. Zero became the symbol for no 'one' at home. In a similar way, the invention of the Fool or the Joker is an essential feature of the tarot cards. It introduces the mercurial into the equation, which is the fundamental ingredient of the unconscious and of human psychology. The unpredictable, which can turn up at any time and in any situation, is the principle of originality, the origin of peculiarity, the riddle of personality.

Having no position requires a certain attitude, what we might call a dis-position, the characteristic of displaced persons. People who reach the depths of themselves, rock bottom, are said to be in touch with the ground of their being. Point zero. Square one. This is what we call 'humility'. Not some hypocritical self-demeaning abasement, but as the word 'humus' originally signified: being earthed, standing squarely on the reality of who we are, and the ground we occupy on planet earth.

Psychologically speaking, when we say there's no one at home, we imply that the person is a simpleton, a fool. 'I've got your number', or 'your number is up' are ways of saying that we know exactly where someone stands, the column in which they are situated, the pigeon-hole, the label, the category, which sums them up.

This card puts us outside such denominations. It doesn't have any fixed place in the sequence, any position in the otherwise exact order of the deck. The Joker is wild. Put him beside card number one, The Magician, and together they become a number ten, which is another circle in The Wheel of Fortune. Put him beside card number two, Wisdom or the

High Priestess, and they become the number twenty, which is the Judgement Seat. Between them they make up the total quantum of what is to be judged in the end. The Fool is an eccentric. Impossible to pin down. If we meet him outside ourselves we become angry, intolerant. The sight of wasters, vagrants, hobos, tramps, hitch-hikers, beggars, clowns, idiots, fills us with fury. These people should be put away, locked up. Why are they permitted to importune us? They shouldn't be here. They make us uncomfortable. They threaten both our security and our obsession about insecurity, a lifetime of making assurance doubly sure. Their nonchalance, insouciance, carefree 'couldn't carelessness' is a challenge to our meticulous defense mechanisms.

The card presents an ambling simpleton, his head in the air, his eyes agog. He carries a staff in one hand and a small bundle with all his belongings slung over his back in the other. He wears the cap and bells of a medieval clown, a tatterdemalion. His feet and his eyes point in different directions. Aimless wandering wherever the spirit moves him. A dog worries him from behind and has torn a large strip from his trousers, exposing one naked haunch. He doesn't seem to notice such details. His vocation is not to be a swatter of flies.

When we meet this card inside ourselves it is terrifying. This is each one of us at our most basic. This is what we are behind all the trappings, the degrees, the success, the wealth, the *curriculum vitae*, the training, the skill, the fame, the rank, the celebrity, kudos, popularity, prestige. And this is what we can be at any time, and in whatever situation the cards may be dealt. The word 'fool' comes from the Latin word 'follis', meaning 'a pair of bellows, a wind-bag'. And as Shakespeare, that great inventor of fools, has said: our little lives are 'sound and fury signifying nothing'. But if we emphasise the last word rather than letting it die away into despair, we detect another dimension to this trump card of our lives. And 'silly' fool is derived from the original Anglo-Saxon word 'saelig', meaning 'happy' or 'blessed': as in 'happy are the poor in spirit'.

The Fool, as point zero, symbolises what is genuine about us. Pure gold. It is who we are when naked. It is us at ground zero, standing inside the first circle of ourselves. It is the integrity of our personality without which any other kind of success, fame, position, wealth, are worthless. It is more important than intelligence, self-control, power, position. To be able to place that card beside ourselves at any moment of our lives and let it superimpose its skeleton on the shape we have become is being real, really being. Such genuineness saves us in whatever situation life throws our way, in whatever order or pattern the cards are dealt. This card tells us that the human capacity for achieving new meaning is linked to our capacity to let life make a fool of us. If we can look into the mirror and recognise the fool, if we can unflinchingly assert that the fool is satisfied, if we can welcome the uninvited guest of ourselves at any moment, even when taken unawares, then there is a possibility that the diamonds are real, the prize genuine, the glitter gold.

But without consultation with the fool, most qualifications are forged, bank notes counterfeit, friendships false. Fool's gold, a fool's errand, a fool's paradise: life achievements of those who never look twice. This card is the gauge, should be the touchstone, the yardstick of what we do and say. Humility in person. Our person. Person, in essence.

THE MAGICIAN

This first card describes the attitude we must adopt, indeed the person we must become, if we are to plumb the secret depths and decode the hidden knowledge that the unconscious contains. The Magician or the Magus is the interpreter. He or she is the ancient Hermes, messenger of the gods, unlocking the treasure trove and bringing forth wisdom old and new. The magician supplies the hermeneutics, a more recent scholarly term, which allows for translation into our everyday lives of the strange symbolic logic of the unconscious. It is not possible for the magus, or for us, to definitively crack the secret code. The unconscious always remains a mystery. But a certain attitude, awareness, intuitive attention is what we must find, and adopt, if we are to undertake this strange but necessary journey. This magus, guru, shaman, who is to dive to the depths and retrieve for us the secret knowledge of our being, has a jaunty look, mostly described by his hat. A sense of humour is essential to this task. The word 'humour' comes from the same root as 'humus' in humility. It is the Latin for earth or ground. We have to be grounded. Both feet securely on the ground.

Look at the card carefully. The Magician is standing at a table. It is a working table. But this is the altar, the anvil, where secret wisdom can be forged. His feet are planted firmly on the ground. One foot is shod in red, the other in blue. Half of him is flesh and blood reality (red), the other half is hidden inspiration (blue). He is a craftsman. His table is a workspace. On it is a satchel, from which he has emptied the instruments of his trade, the various games of chance. These represent the bag of tricks that every culture accumulates in the service of its hidden wisdom. Cups with dice, the four suit cards of the minor tarot pack, what we would call in our card games today, diamonds, hearts, clubs and spades. In the tarot pack these are cups and coins, swords and clubs. In his left hand is a wand or a stick, in his right a golden coin.

On his head he wears a lemniscate hat. 'Lemniscate' is a scientific term adapted to describe designs like figures of eight turned sideways, which have always represented infinity – the sky is the limit where the work of the magician is concerned. The term has been adopted from chemistry to describe certain kinds of rather flamboyant hats, such as those worn at weddings or by musketeers. The Magician's hat has a blood-coloured rim. His knowledge is more than scientific.

Although he is plying his trade, his gaze is in another direction, absorbed by something else. This describes a kind of attention or awareness that is essential for his art, as it is for spiritual activity of any kind, from art to contemplation. Awareness without concentration: uncomplicated presence of mind. This first arcanum – the principle underlying the other 21 major arcana, teaches us the essential rapport that should exist between personal effort and spiritual reality. The mystic must be, in a certain way, laid back. One of the golden rules of all searches for wisdom is contained in a line from the *Corpus Hermeticum*:

Learn at first concentration without effort; transform work into play; make every yoke you accept easy and every burden you carry light!

Secret wisdom requires that its bearers be detached. Relaxed and taut at the same time, like a musical instrument. There is a fanatical zeal, an intensity, which many searchers in the spiritual life presume necessary for such exploration. Quite the contrary. Gluttons, misers, control freaks, religious maniacs do achieve quite remarkable concentration, which is what we term obsession. This is the imposter that our present card exposes. The effort required in the search is similar to a game. Cards are an appropriate display case. There is a particular kind of concentration applicable to play. Take the example of a tightrope walker in a circus. Only this particular kind of concentration can work. If you concentrate on each step you take, you are bound to fall. What must be fostered is the intelligence of the rhythmic system, the intense but unconscious participation of both the respiratory and circulatory systems, which replace the working of the brain during such acrobatic feats.

The lemniscate hat is a symbol also of such circulation: eternal rhythm in which our attention to the divine becomes as natural as breathing, taking its cue from the beating of the heart.

We attach ourselves to the breathing of the Spirit, and our internal circulation begins to pulse according to the impulse of this higher rhythm. Our breathing is infiltrated by another breath.

The French name at the bottom of this card is *Le Bateleur*, which means the Juggler. The juggler creates magic patterns in space and time.

In 1892, the French writer Anatole France (1844–1924) wrote *Le Jongleur de Notre Dame*, 'Our Lady's Juggler'. The story is a traditional French tale, but his version became the one best known and loved. Set in the fourteenth century at Cluny, a Benedictine abbey in east central France, which lasted from 910 until its closing in 1790, the story tells of a humble juggler named Barnaby, who in time of need is sheltered by the monks. The members of this particular monastic order are painters, musicians, poets, who make magnificent offerings to demonstrate their religious devotion. Barnaby makes the only contribution he can: he juggles before the statue of the Virgin, who by a miracle stoops to wipe his brow before the scandalised bystanders can remove him.

This first card shows us how to play the real game of tarot. It is a mysterious source of wisdom. Mysticism is the source and root of all religion. Without it there is no real contact with God, and without such immediate and living contact at every moment, religion of whatever kind is dead. The Magician, who is the source of secret wisdom, is of necessity a mystic. The essence of mysticism is creative activity of a certain kind. The mystic has to be alive, living the life of resurrection: that is why in this first card the person stands upright. Mysticism itself is pure movement. It is rhythmical attention that requires neither image nor word. The tips of the Magician's fingers are touching something – we have to return to the original religious element or source in ourselves. The only prerequisite for prayer is our readiness for this presence of God, our total attention, our simple turned-towardness, our unreserved spontaneity, or 'Ekagra', which means something like 'one-pointedness'. We are there, we are ready, we are waiting. The art of mysticism is touch, which can be without any form, colour, or sound. Secret wisdom is gleaned through such spiritual touch or intuition. Mystics through the ages have used the image of a kiss to describe the way we touch God and the way God touches us. This first card shows us the way.

THE HIGH PRIESTESS

Card number two represents the kind of wisdom required in our search. If the Magician represents the way, the High Priestess is the truth. This is Sophia, the kind of wisdom we must have in order to approach the mysteries hidden since the beginning of time. The woman on the card is seated. The word 'sophia' means 'seat of wisdom'. She carries a book in her lap, which is opened by both her hands. This book is the distilled embodiment of her life and being as a channel of wisdom, as an incarnation of obedience to the Word. On her head she wears a triple tiara, which represents the threefold wisdom that filters from above into her opened heart and soul and mind, until it becomes flesh in her and then is reborn as Word once again in the holy book. The three levels are inspiration, then reflection and memory, followed by active expression in her own words. It is a process similar to giving birth. Her work is, at every level, inspired. The card shows very graphically the descent of revelation from the small uppermost circle on her tiara down to the open book on her knees. She is seated in a way that graphically depicts relationship between the vertical and the horizontal: the circling, descending spiral rings of the tiara that covers her head and the arrival of this into a horizontal and outward plane in the square pages of the book.

Such is the way in which tradition is born. It is necessary to be seated. This describes an active-passive state of being that allows for attentive listening in silence. The complete figure is the human being as attentive ear. 'I am all ears', we say when attentive to what another person says. The book lying open at the base of this waterfall allows the wisdom to be handed over, handed on. But a book never contains the fullness of the wisdom that is embodied in this extraordinary person. Not all the books in the world could contain the sum total of this mystery.

At the level of the unconscious, this card portrays a link with that underworld that psychology tries to reach. This world is beyond the reach of our everyday consciousness and any attempt by the very masculine tools of reason to force a way in is inadequate. Such wisdom is inaccessible to scientific examination. It contains both our hidden potentiality and our darkest, most primeval layers of personality. We glimpse it through dreams; we sense a possible weave in its texture from strange incidents that happen, unusual coincidences that impose themselves. It requires a great deal of patience and long-term vigilance at the various hidden exits from the underground network before we detect a possible pattern that can eventually become visible in the workaday world. This silent and still figure of the second card bears witness to a history being woven through the vicissitudes of life, which comes from an invisible source and which can only be sensed by us as the red thread of our destiny through intuition and meditation.

The High Priestess (in some versions she is the Popess or female pope) is essentially feminine. This wisdom is attainable through the feminine principle, whether it be in a man or a woman. Such a principle is underprivileged and suppressed to a great extent in the world we have inherited. Its liberation is a work to be achieved as much in the lives of men as it is in the lives of women. The woman sits on a throne, and for the reign of such wisdom to become explicit, effective and available it is important that this High Priestess be released from the depths of the unconscious and established on an equal footing with her masculine counterpart so prevalent and so obvious in our world of science and technology.

In the realms of science and of worldly wisdom our knowledge comes from the opposite direction. There is nothing in the mind, Aristotle would say, apart from what we receive through our five senses. The external world becomes conceptualised (which comes from the same word we use for conceiving a child), through bombardment of the brain with electro-chemical currents transmitted from the world outside us. We are informed by our overworked sense organs, which transmit to our central nervous systems a continuous stream of sense impressions translated into electrical currents that feed the brain. We learn that nature has a horror of emptiness (*horror vacui*). Nothing is more detrimental to science than empty-headedness. Nor do you get much done if you sit around in silence all day with your eyes closed and your brain unoccupied.

In the realms of the Spirit, the opposite is true: the Spirit has a horror of fullness. To receive the secret wisdom, we have to open ourselves and empty ourselves; once this evacuation of the ego is complete, our personality and our total being, body and spirit, become vehicles for the mystery which is beyond us. The source of such knowledge is above and beyond. Garnering it requires the suspension of the natural process of science, the temporary closing down of the sensory conveyor belt. The tiara as a visual image is almost like a closely fitting suction pump, which achieves the seamless connection between the Spirit from above and the spirit of the woman herself. It is conception by spirit and by water. Infusion takes place through the pinpoint at the top. Her spirit becomes divine Breath, which replaces her own personal activity, and her inner stillness is the pool that acts as mirror to the Divine. Such impregnation is anathema to the intellectual trend-setters of our newly inherited century. The tarot cards contain not only a secret wisdom but a very ancient and unfashionable depiction of a way of knowing, a method of understanding, considered by many to be obsolete or unacceptable.

This second card is about spiritual listening; the first card is about spiritual touch. The first card showed us the way; this one shows us the truth.

III

L'IMPÉRATRICE

THE EMPRESS

The third and fourth cards are mother and father archetypes on the grand scale. This card is the Arcanum of fecundity. Love is the source of all life, biological, religious, artistic, intellectual. But this powerful source can drown as well as deliver us. This card represents us as possible life submerged in a womb of darkness, amoebas fighting for survival down the rapids of the unconscious. We have an ambivalent relationship with the tarot of the Empress. She can be Madonna, our mother and our queen, symbol of life, of sweetness and of hope, or she can be the goddess Kali, bloodthirsty wife of Shiva, the terrible mother of smothering love. This devouring aspect becomes apparent even in the workaday world whenever, according to Sallie Nichols,[1] woman neglects her true kingdom, which is relationship, and becomes power hungry. Then she becomes truly a man-eater. The Empress has swapped the power of love for the love of power.

However, in this tarot card we are dealing not with the world of men and women in the socio-political dimension, but with male and female principles deeply embedded in the human make-up of every one of us. Our lives are a struggle between such principles and our goal is integration: the harmonious balance between the conscious and the unconscious, between the masculine and the feminine. It takes us many years of outlandish projecting on to the innocent bystanders who make up the players in our game of cards before we can see them simply as human beings.

This card can be interpreted as Black Witch, Wicked Stepmother, Ugly Sister – all those readymade personas that we pitch at people who have the appropriate features to which we can affix our posters. In her negative aspect the Empress can be portrayed as a dragon who guards the golden fleece, the pearl of great price – whatever it is we want from life. As such she represents, again in the words of Sallie Nichols, 'the devouring regressive aspect of unconscious nature' which each one of us as the Hero (which is the symbolic way of representing our humanity striving for consciousness) must slay to obtain that freedom which means transcending mere animal existence (MT 97).

In its positive representation, this card represents the balance which we must achieve between our conscious and unconscious selves and the spiritual relationship we must develop in order to effect this harmony. The card shows the Empress swathed in garments of flowing red and blue as if emerging from the earth, keeping her head above water. We also have to keep ourselves afloat in the swamp of unconscious forces that both give us life and yet threaten to overwhelm us. The two-layered crown that the Empress wears represents the necessity for us to attach ourselves to the higher will which both gave us life and seeks to guide us to fulfilment.

The sceptre shows, especially in its connected halves at the top, the union of the two wills pictured in the crown, now become a living reality. The top half, or the cup surmounted by the cross and turned downwards, is the divine will; the cup supported by the staff and turned upwards represents our human will. One looks like an acorn, the other like a drop of blood.

The aim of these combined wills, their goal, is represented by the shield. An eagle heralds liberating action, restoration of freedom, emblem of resurrection. The purpose is to give us such freedom: freedom to see, hear, walk, live, as inheritors of that most abundant life which is ours for the taking if we can rid ourselves of the chains that hold us back.

The throne on which the Empress is seated represents that place from which we all come. It is earthbound and claustrophobic, representing all that is deprived of liberty and bound by necessity. The throne has a back that looks like two wings. It is almost as if a spell had been cast on them and they had been turned into stone, immobilised. But they still have the shape of wings and are still capable of flying if the right energy is applied and their paralysis cured.

This third card, like the third person of the Trinity, brings life. We belong to the tree of life. Life itself is a series of miracles. From the root right up to the topmost leaves, each evolutionary step is a choice. Nature is giving birth to us at each moment of our lives. We have the choice to become whatever we want to become. This requires an osmosis similar to that required of the caterpillar who chooses to develop into a butterfly. You rose from the dead on the day that you were conceived; you can do it again – not just after your death but at every moment of your life that you choose to invest with such consciousness.

Card 2 showed us how to perceive the Spirit. The third arcanum of the tarot shows us the first step we must take to bring this new awareness into our lives. Now we must take possession of our own lives, by becoming fully human and freely connecting that humanity with God.

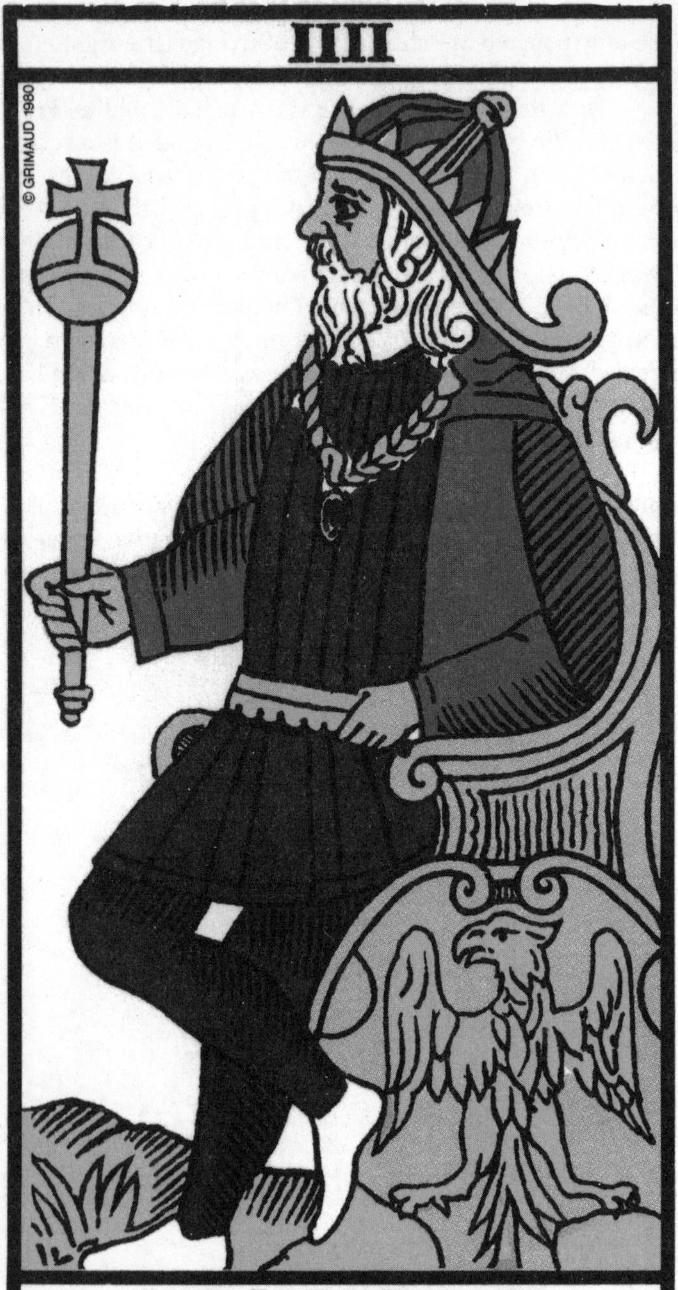
IIII
© GRIMAUD 1980
L'EMPEREUR

ΙΕ EMPEROR

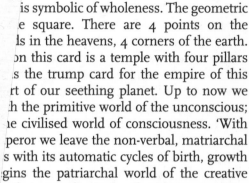

is symbolic of wholeness. The geometric
e square. There are 4 points on the
ls in the heavens, 4 corners of the earth.
on this card is a temple with four pillars
s the trump card for the empire of this
rt of our seething planet. Up to now we
h the primitive world of the unconscious;
ie civilised world of consciousness. 'With
peror we leave the non-verbal, matriarchal
s with its automatic cycles of birth, growth
gins the patriarchal world of the creative
word, which initiates the masculine rule of spirit over nature.
This ruler is an embodiment of the Logos, or rational principle,
which is an aspect of the Father archetype. He orders our
thoughts and energies, connecting them with reality in a
practical way' (SN, 103).

The figure on this card wears no armour and carries no
sword. He is neither standing nor sitting. He is on sentry duty,
bound to his post. Note the size and strength of his right hand,
which carries the sceptre, and compare it with his left hand
holding his belt. His kingdom is hard won. His right hand has
doubled in size from overuse. The struggle whereby we reach
consciousness involves almost superhuman feats of strength,
'for Mother Nature guards her kingdom jealously' (SN, 104).

This Emperor has established in himself a fourfold
emptiness: he has renounced the movement of his legs, which
form a cross somewhat similar to that of the Hanged Man in
card 12; he has renounced the free movement of his arms; and
through the helmet-like covering of his head which is his crown
he has renounced freedom of intellectual movement. He has
renounced his personal mission in favour of the throne. He is
not here in his own name but in the name of the throne. He is
anonymous. The shield is there, as in the previous card, a

rampant eagle, still signifying freedom, fullness of being, resurrection, but it belongs to the throne, not to his person. This is why he is Emperor, why he has authority. He has made a place in himself for the source of all authority. He has excavated within himself those archaeological openings that are the source of law and order.

The Emperor of the fourth card is alone, without court or retinue. His throne is not in a room but out in the open. Alone under the open sky, he is responsible for achieving the personal connection between the will of God and the way things happen on earth. Through his authority the kindom may come. His power is effected by the contraction of his personal forces. Note how tightly the belt is drawn around his waist. His rule is achieved by voluntary immobility at his post. By nailing himself to the seat of wisdom he can become the channel for such authority within our world.

God governs the world by authority, and not by force. Everything that took place in the story of the prodigal son, except for his return to his father, was clearly contrary to the will of the father. Humanity is solely responsible for history. It is not God who has willed it to be such. God is crucified in our world. He is powerless. The future of the world is up to us. If we want to know how God might want that future to be, we have to post sentries who can listen for instructions. Otherwise the juggernaut is driven by whoever happens to be at the wheel.

The first act of all was not an act of revelation but one of limitation. In other words, in order to create the world ex nihilo, God had first to bring the void into existence. He had to withdraw within in order to create a mystical space without, a space without his presence – the void. The void is the place of origin of freedom, of an ex-istence, which means literally 'to stand outside'. We exist as absolute potentiality, not in any way determined. This is precisely why no one can predict the future, because the future is in our hands. We make the future happen. All created things carry within them something of the void and something of the divine spark. Their existence, their freedom, is a result of the void within them. Their essence, their spark of love, is the divine within them.

The card of the Emperor shows us how we can reconnect with the love of God. The throne is the post of the representative of humanity; it could be, through his good offices, the throne of the kingdom. Such a reign would involve the re-humanisation of all elements of human nature and their return to their true essence. The essence of humanity is love. The existence of humanity requires the void. The Emperor in each one of us is the card we play to make that vital connection. The Emperor reigns by pure authority; he reigns over free beings, not by the sword but by means of the sceptre.

The sceptre is the key symbol. It graphically portrays the vital connection which is a lightning conductor of the power that saves. It is divided into two pieces. Held up from below it is a cup or goblet with a very long stem. Filling this goblet is a drop from above surmounted by a cross. Such is the blood transfusion that can alter the natural flow of human nature in its biological journey from birth to death. A vertical intervention can stem that flow and insert the time warp of resurrection. Through the ministrations of the anointed one, a kingdom under the aegis of that new commandment can be maintained, but it is a hands-on, minute-by-minute maintenance programme that requires the presence at all times of a sentry willingly chained to that post.

We have now been introduced to the way, the truth, and the life.

V

LE · PAPE

V

THE POPE

The fifth card brings this first quintet to completion. It represents, as the number suggests, a quintessence of the spiritual quest. Just as we have five senses and five fingers with which to probe the world around us, so this pentagram will be significant in probing the world of the Spirit. The Pope is called pontifex, which in Latin means bridge-builder between two worlds. This card represents a blessing or benediction. Benediction is nothing less than the power of God. Whoever is entitled to give such a blessing is putting into action divine power. Such exercise of the divine will transcends all individuality of thought and of will-power, either in the one who is blessing, or in those being blessed. This card presents us with an essentially sacerdotal act.

The design of the card describes a circular movement of prayer and benediction passing from the left-hand side of the card to the right. Two disciples or acolytes kneel before the Pope. The one on the left has his hands raised in prayer; the one on the right has his hands lowered and open to receive the blessing from the Pope's right hand. Moving up from the head of the supplicant is a triple cross, which carries the prayer heavenward. A similar movement downwards from the descending tiara through the red folding robes of the Pope leads the blessing of his right hand to the head of the other acolyte. The three heads and the two pillars of the throne behind the Pope make up the sign of the pentagram. On their own the two pillars and the tiara form a tryptich, which mirrors the parallel lines of the triple cross, which in turn designates the three layers of the tiara. This mitre-shaped crown, decorated with three-leaved shamrock templates beside what look like keyhole openings, has the appearance of a beehive. It is indeed a beehive of the invisible. The complex weave of the Trinity issues through the blessing into several streams of prayer: Thy kingdom come as addressed to the Father; Thy will be done as expressed through the Son; and Give us this day our daily bread as uttered by, with and through the Holy Spirit.

It is only the pentagram of the five wounds that is the effective sign of personal sacred magic. Under this sign, the benediction flows. Each of the wounds of Christ are effective antidotes against the five dark currents of human motivation: the desire to be great, the desire to take (the prerogative of the right hand), the desire to keep (prerogative of the left hand), the desire to advance at the expense of others (prerogative of the right foot), the desire to hold on to, at the expense of others (prerogative of the left foot). The five wounds of Christ were a five sense breakthrough into our world of the greedy senses and covetous limbs. His wounds are five vacuities which result in the five currents of the human will being filled from above by absolutely pure will, the will of God. This is the principle of the magic of the pentagram of the five wounds.

A wound is a door. The eye, for instance, is a wound covered by a mobile skin which we call an eyelid. Our eyes are open wounds. So are our other senses. They are wounds through which the world imposes itself on us. The five senses are organs of perception, not of action. They are passive receptors. The five organs of action, on the other hand, are our two legs, our two arms, and our head. These must develop analogous wounds that will become the stigmata of our alignment to the cross of the divine will. The head, however, does not bear the fifth wound, as we know from the paradigm of the Christian mystery. It bears the crown of thorns. These are the nails of objectivity. They are represented on the tiara as nails and wounds.

The fifth wound, as is suggested by the fifth card of the major arcana of the tarot, is where the fingers of the pope are pointing: it is the wound of organic humility, which replaces the natural current of the will-to-greatness. This wound penetrates from the right-hand side. The twentieth century made us more aware than ever of the currents of natural energy that normally motivate us and spur us to action. Three philosophers each suggested one of these instincts as the primary motivation for everything we do or say: Freud nominated sex, Nietzsche suggested the will to power, Marx thought money made the world go round.

In a corresponding assignation from the other side of the spectrum, generations of spiritual seekers stemmed the flow of the natural currents of selfishness by taking three corresponding vows. The vow of poverty attacks greed and rivets the desire to take and to keep, which are the natural movements of our two hands. Poverty undermines the tendencies of the thief: male to seize, female to keep indefinitely. The vow of chastity tried to wound the beast of lust, and pin down the limbs of the hunter, namely our two feet. Chastity keeps in check the instincts of the hunter in the human being, of which the masculine is inclined to pursue game and the feminine to set traps. Finally the vow of obedience attacks the central urge and rivets the will-to-greatness of the heart, which in the masculine principle thinks itself great in its own eyes, whereas in the feminine it tries to make itself great in the sight of others.

Whatever the method, the mission of spiritual leadership, as depicted in this fifth card, is to make sure that spiritual obedience, poverty and chastity – free and holy – do not disappear from the world. Because without at least one person who carries this spiritual stigmata, there is no guarantee that the flow of grace from above can reach the earth below. The only wound through which such power can flow is the freely opened heart and will of an authentic lover of God. Such a person is the one represented in this card. No amount of worldly pomp or pageantry can create such an office. The only lightning conductor that can harness the power of God is the loving will of a genuine pontifex. It does not matter how we break down these walls between the two sides, it may require quite different kinds of wounding in the case of each individual. However, what is ungainsayable is this: The bridge is created through the open wounds on both sides.

The two fingers of the pope which point to the wounded heart also hide from sight the three remaining fingers, which represent the three persons of the Trinity waiting in secret to enter our hearts through the Holy Spirit, sometimes described as *digitus dei*, the finger of God.

The triple cross of the pope's crosier is the victory sign of the Divine breakthrough. It is the power of salvation. So potent is this staff that no human being should touch it without a gloved hand. The freedom we have been given is so powerful and so dangerous that it can lead us through every one of our five senses to a hell of our own construction. That is what freedom means: the free choice of surrender to heaven or construction of hell from our own sweating selves. The secret wisdom hidden from the beginning of time is the mystery of God's love for us. And so powerful is this secret wisdom that the five gates of hell shall never prevail against the formula of the five wounds.

THE LOVER

We only begin to live when we fall in love. Before that time we are like the sleeping beauty, asleep and waiting to be awoken. Subjective life begins when we fall in love. The sun in this card is replaced by Cupid with his bow and arrow. A new day has dawned, the first day of the beginning of our new life. Everything has faded into the background, nothing now exists except the one we love. All time is impatience that is not spent in this presence; all space is a desert and a prison that separates us from our loved one.

We have been stricken. The poisoned dart of Cupid's arrow has killed off the world that used to hold our interest. The arrow in the card is aimed at the heart. Vulnerable, shredded, bepatched, the victim stands in the middle. The youth is flanked by two women, one younger, one older. The older woman holds his gaze and touches his shoulder somewhat possessively, pointing towards his head. The younger woman touches his heart. What looks like his hand, although it seems to have invaded her sleeve, is groping towards her midriff, even as his eyes are hypnotised by the other. He is stuck like Balaam's ass between two delights: consciously he seems to veer towards the older woman, whereas his body language swivels towards the younger. He is divided in two: to choose either and leave the other means leaving one half of himself behind. The combinations of this triangle are interchangeable. In fact the younger pair are look-alikes. They could be brother and sister. The person in the centre could as easily be a young woman flanked by an older and a younger man. The game is played in this configuration no matter who turns up to fill each role.

We are no longer in the world of spiritual striving; we have landed on earth and are presented with a very human problem. A young man is involved with two women. His two naked feet are firmly planted on the ground. Narcissism means that we nearly always begin love by falling for ourselves. The first person we fall in love with is often strangely familiar. And that word 'familiar' implies that it remains in the family. Somewhere in the ideal archetype of my perfect partner is a mixture in variant proportions of my mother and myself. The title of the card in French is a revealing anomaly. The word begins as a singular and ends as a plural. The L' at the outset suggests one lover (a definite article); the X at the end spells at least two. There is always this triangle when we fall in love. The card shows two women: the one we are afraid to let go of is our mother; the one we are afraid to move towards is our dream.

We learnt from Pythagoras that the triangle was the first geometrical figure symbolising a fundamental human reality. Both of these women are essential to his being in different ways. If he can stand his ground and endure the tension, he can interiorise what the significance of each is for his own life and growth. If he chooses one rather than the other, his deepest undiscovered needs will always remain with the woman he left behind. He will be manipulated all his life by the possibility he never explored. Enduring might release him from the magic spell of both: the elastic bands that fasten him to each in uncontrollable thraldom could then snap back and settle into the disentangled tendrils of his own interiority. 'Newly emerging consciousness, like physical distance, often produces a kind of double vision, so that what appears in dreams or other symbolic material at first as "those women" will later come into focus as one individual' (SN, 131). It is obviously in the interest of the lover to wait patiently until this happens. Otherwise he wanders from one to the other, from one relationship to the next, never finding satisfaction in love or love in satisfaction. At the beginning he is possessed by both these women, and their possessiveness only reinforces his paralysis. If he goes with one, the other is bound to haunt him psychologically for the rest of his life. Anything of ourselves that we leave behind in the unconscious will needle us and destabilise any later relationship. 'By eliminating its [love's] stresses and tension we may be losing an initiatory rite of great importance in the development of human consciousness' (SN, 133). This young man needs exorcism, which can only be performed from inside himself. He alone holds the key to his own prison house, the cure for his addiction. Unless he finds it he will remain a cripple, proud of his crutches, lurching intermittently from one hallucinatory lover to the next, or using both to hold himself up. At the symbolic level this card is clear: in order to be our own person we have to free ourselves from the regressive pull of whatever womb seeks to contain us. We have to cut that umbilical cord and step into our own autonomy. This will, like any birth, require bloodshed, but it is the only entry to life.

Whereas the Arcana of the Pope offered us the way into the life of the Spirit, this first card of the second quintet points the way towards maturity of psychological and emotional life. The double vision presented here is proof that the source of such emotion is the search for wholeness, for total vision. Both these women are necessary to the longing of the lover; neither must be allowed to stop him from following these parallel energies to the point where the parallel lines meet. The number of this card, six, is also a number of completion. Completion is not perfection, neither is it termination. Chastity is not possible unless we love the totality of our own being. Symbolically six is a star composed of two triangles. The masculine triangle of fire and the feminine triangle of water reach a configuration in Solomon's star, which connects the heavens and the earth. In this larger context, the antinomies of the love triangle depicted here are defused in a more cosmic geometry, whose maxim is: as above, so below. The mystic marriage of heaven and earth is the goal. Inside ourselves this is mirrored by the marriage of conscious and unconscious. Whatever decision this young man takes and whichever lover he chooses, he takes himself with him. This reality cannot be shed. And unless this self achieves the freedom that is the crown and the goal of every life worth living, it will be incapable of sustaining long-term relationship with any other person, whoever they may be.

VII

LE CHARIOT

THE CHARIOT

N ow we are on our chariot and ready to begin the journey of life. We are represented in this card by a young prince or king in a four-poster carriage, complete with sceptre and crown. Is this not the same youth who had just been struck by Cupid in the card of love? Again we must remind ourselves that this is not a discriminatory exercise, that in the archetypal world of the tarot 'the Hero' is representative of each and every one of us, male or female, as the personal principle of our individual lives. In the depths of our psyche there is no such thing as 'I'; there it is all 'we', and 'I' am the sum total of all of these; and each one of the divisibles is both male and female. However, the fundamental question for whoever we are is this: Are we going to be the hero of our own life, or are we going to allow someone else to occupy that position? Am I in the driving seat when it comes to my own destination? This young man is the preview to our movie.

His sceptre tilts towards his head on which he wears a crown, which suggests the fealty upon which his flimsy dynasty is based. But the card is divided very exactly in half. The lintel of the balcony is the cut-off point for the puppet show above where our prince assumes the role of both Punch and Judy in the pocket theatre he chooses to call his life. Notice the two faces embedded in the shoulders of his cape. They are the standard masks for tragedy and comedy, identifying his reign as a drama of his own composition. This is a subjective world complete with canopy upheld by the four cardinal virtues which will ensure his reign. The curtained canopy cuts him off from the wider world, and, like King Canute, he can order away the waves of misfortune, or, like the King of Spain, who was playing billiards with his butler when the revolutionary hordes invaded the palace, he can ask: 'Have those people got permission to be in here?'

Because his top-storey emporium is only half the picture, underneath the scene is dominated by two colourful prancing chargers. In the whole rectangular perspective, the king has become a centaur, that mythological creature, half human, half horse. But situated in the square box overhead, he has cut himself off, has established himself as superior to this equestrian undercarriage. His impotence is obvious when we notice that there are no reins in his hands, that the horses he is meant to be driving are without bridle or bit. Meanwhile, in the menagerie underneath, the wheels of the chariot are askew and would seem to be pointing in the opposite direction to the pair of lively horses, one red, one blue, which are also moving away from each other. This horse-power is symbolic of human motivation. Horses represent our passionate nature: there is a spiritual as well as a physical dimension to such movement. This can translate itself psychologically into anger and lust for the red horse, melancholy and depression for the blue. Many songs and stories have identified the colours. 'O Heart! Heart! Heart! O the bleeding drops of red!' or 'You ain't been blue, till you've had that mood indigo.' Both passions pull in different directions. Even more distressing is having no way of directing or controlling.

The card is not called either 'The Driver' or 'The Horses'. The problem is falsified if we accept the logic of our hero and the statement made by his architecture and apparel. The seventh arcana is the first one named after a machine. All six previous cards were persons. Here in the second quintet we enter the world of organization, of structures, of technology. The Chariot describes the way we move forward if we wish to live a truly human life. And the first thing to be understood is that we are hybrid creatures, that we are half human and half horse, and that both of these halves make us fully human. Unless we cater adequately for the horsepower of our every movement, we have failed to assume our humanity. The orthodoxy of humanity imposes its natural law on any institution that seeks to guide or control it. If we fail to take what we are into account, if we cease to be attentive horse-whisperers, we may be very effective legislators and highly successful organisers but we are not providing for the constituents we were appointed to serve.

The number of this card is 7: seven is the sacred number in several cultures for unity within complexity. The 7 ages of man, the 7 sacraments, the 7 deadly sins, the 7 seals in the Book of Revelation, the 7 chakras – all betoken an achievement of totality, of completeness, which is probably its combination of the numbers three and four, the triangle within the square. Even in our own very materialistic culture there are 7 days of the week and 7 wonders of the world, and unless we include every one of these places and these times in whatever calculations we make and whatever structures or technology we devise, we are not going to get ourselves to wherever it is we were intended to go. The 7 elements in this card: the driver, the two horses and the four pillars upholding his canopy, need to be rearranged in an order that does justice to all of them. If the driver simply moves forward at speed, he is riding for a fall. He is also endangering anyone he meets on the way. We cannot, as we say, ride roughshod over people. Nor can he unhitch either of the horses and continue on his way. If he does, he is leaving behind the other half of the problem. And that, as we again put it in common parlance, is a horse of a different colour.

The SM emblazoned on the front describes the opposites that need to be combined, a symbiosis of conflicting needs required to harness creatively the turbulent violence of instinctual nature. Domination is not the answer; nor is craven submission. Discipline comes from harmonious involvement in appropriate and spontaneous activity. When the centaur knows where a centaur should be going and why, the chariot will move forward with all hands and hoofs on deck. The person in charge must change paradigm from a king holding a golden sceptre to a conductor wielding a delicate baton, as he or she guides each member of a dedicated orchestra. You can bring a horse to water but you can't make it into an outboard engine. Horses have their own ways of becoming human.

JUSTICE

We need to do 'justice' to the totality of our situation. This has always been regarded as one of the cardinal virtues in whatever system of behaviour we devise for ourselves and for others. From Aristotle to the American Declaration of Independence to the UN Charter of Human Rights, justice has been the primary concern of all legislators for human well-being. The card here is number 8. The Greeks identified this number with justice because it comprises equal divisions of even numbers. In the Arabic numerals it assumes the shape of infinity or eternity, which is, once again, the lemniscate shape which we have already identified in the Magician's hat.

The card shows a woman seated on a golden throne holding in her right hand a sword held perpendicularly, in line with the pillar of her throne and the axis of the weighing scales, which she holds near her heart in her bent left hand. The balance is in its most simple form: a vertical fixed axis with a beam forming a cross horizontal to this, with two scales suspended at the end of the beam. The two golden orbs acting as containers on each side are suspended by strings. The seated woman seems to emerge like a petalled flower from the golden earth. Her seven chakras are open and aligned, reaching with a final flourish the three-tiered crown, which opens in a golden-toothed awning piercing the sky. Justice for the medieval world was balance or harmony. The Golden Mean was that delicate path we must tread between extremes of behaviour or temperament.

However, there is something smug about this solitary figure sitting in such unruffled equanimity holding her perfectly balanced weighing scales and her perpendicular sword. It is much easier to be just when one is on one's own. The problems of justice only reveal themselves when you are trying to arbitrate between people with conflicting interests or views. This figure seems to have struck a beautiful and effective balance between the blue of her outer garment and the red of the inner one. These are the colours of the two horses in the previous tarot card. Her elegant shape is like an eight-sided octagon, corresponding to the number of her office. She has achieved a harmonious balance between the outer world of her body and the inner world of her spirit. Her sword is not a weapon, it is a symbol and it points upwards in the direction of heaven. Her eyes stare straight ahead rather than looking either at the sword or at the scales. It is an impersonal gaze. The delicate cups of the weighing scales, which are feminine in form, are exactly even, causing the horizontal connecting bar to form a cross with the vertical masculine form of the phallic sword. She wears a helmet-like headgear, which corresponds to the sword. This has been called a walled crown and corresponds to the back of her throne, which has all the appearance of a wall or an apse. She is guardian of the law, of the city and eventually of civilisation.

All of which suggests, also, that the balance being achieved is that between the masculine and feminine principles. If we take each card as an archetypal milestone in our journey through life, then this is about doing yourself justice rather than doing justice in the world. It is getting your own house in order and defending yourself against the heathens, barbarians, pagans or *perioikoi*, meaning those who are outside, extramural, beyond the possibility of citizenship. The emphasis is on the right-hand side, which holds the sword, the maintainer of law and order. It is a justice based on rational, conscious decisions, based upon reasonable judgements, after critical examination and assessment of all the objective data. This sword on the right-hand side is double-edged. It follows the patriarchal pattern of card number four, the Emperor, and occupies space eight, which is double that number. So, it is a cut-and-dried exercise of the law; and matters of the heart or areas of intuition are not likely to get adequate or sympathetic hearing. The equilibrium is pictured in the weighing scales, and the power to restore it whenever necessary is symbolised by the sword. This is rough justice and can only serve as a step along the way between lynch law and the discernment of wisdom. The justice of law needs to be tempered by the equity of grace. Into the inexorable weighing scales the quality of mercy must be poured. Justice, as central figure in the card, is enthroned as rigidly and as inflexibly as her sword; the opposite pans of her scales are held apart on an equally inflexible crossbar. These instruments are man-made devices for discrimination and measurement. This is Solomon cutting the baby in two with his sword to give an equal share to both contestants claiming to be its mother. Justice in this representation is from above; it does not get personally involved. It is an allegorical figure, neither human nor divine.

VIIII

© GRIMAUD 1980

L'HERMITE

THE HERMIT

Nine is the last single digit before returning to zero to start the second decimal phase of our wanderings. The Hermit is the Fool more wordly wise. This card represents the final stage of the first half of the tarot journey. It ends the solar expedition and begins the lunar phase. We have seen the front of the tapestry on the way out and are being introduced to the obverse side on the way back. The inside view is not as beautiful but it is more instructive; we see how the threads were woven through the apparently seamless design in front.

Nine, like five, symbolises a totality, a wholeness. Ninepins, the traditional game, has eight courtiers surrounding a 'king' in the middle. Queen Maeve of the Irish *Táin Bó Cuailnge* travelled with two chariots before her, two chariots behind her, two chariots on either side, and her own chariot in the centre making up a company of nine. May day, summer's eve, the return of order to a world of chaos, the dawn of a new and orderly day, is also associated with nine. The number is connected with the *Bealtaine* fire in Scotland, Ireland, Wales and Scandinavia, where it was lit by nine men with nine branches from nine different trees. The card shows a monk, like Lao-tzu, whose name means 'old man', embodying a wisdom, not to be found in books: a wisdom both elemental and ageless, represented by the fire in his lamp.

Unlike the Pope and the Emperor, the Hermit has no throne. He has swapped the gilded sceptre for a sturdy walking stick. Like the Fool, he is a wanderer, an itinerant like ourselves, walking common ground with us, wandering through the world. He is what every 'fool' and each one of us should become. He has swapped the Fool's cap for a cowl and has adopted a more measured pace than his younger prototype. He is not looking over his shoulder: he has assimilated the experiences of his past. He is looking forward, calmly and unflinchingly, towards a future lit up step by step in the dim circumspect light of a friar's lantern. This tiny particular lamp represents personal wisdom, not universal law. The design, features, and colours of the card betoken a pragmatic approach to truth rather than an abstract or philosophical one. Such wisdom is not found in libraries; it is distilled in broken hearts. The Hermit's tranquil demeanour results from individual insight. It is the surefootedness of the mystic rather than the assimilated security of religious dogma. The flame burning inside the lamp is that intimate core of meaning which warms the spirit of thoroughly examined human life. It names the unexamined life as not worth living, the unlived life not worth examining. Deep furrows in the brow shape efforts made to come to terms with a universe into which we have been ploughed.

Around the flickering flame of wisdom are wisely inserted shutters creating a storm lantern, protecting both ourselves and the tiny fire. Fire of any kind is potentially dangerous. It must be controlled in order to be useful. Out of control it burns up, destroys. These shutters are made of gold. Gold is the symbol of wisdom distilled. One particular shutter is red: the colour of our flesh-and-blood humanity. The light being thrown from this magic lantern is a mixture of passion and compassion distilled from the experience of a lifetime. Because it is lived and distilled by a particular individual, it is life-sized, credible, and available to all. This charism is to lead with the kindly light of one's own searching humanity, using the light of one's heart to guide the way.

This familiar stranger embodies both aspects of our being. The flowing beard suggests masculinity, the positive 'yang' energy of the Chinese tradition. The flowing robes and gentle expression encapsulate the earthed and more feminine 'yin'.

Lamp, mantle and staff: these betoken light shining in darkness; freedom from collective truisms and borrowed prejudices; all three feet squarely on the ground. He advances only after trying out the ground ahead through immediate experience. The number nine could be three syntheses of three antinomies. Tomberg suggests that 'The Hermit of the ninth Card is the Christian Hermeticist, who represents the "inner work of nine", the work of realising the supremacy of the heart in the human being – in familiar traditional terms: the "work of salvation" – because the "salvation of the soul" is the restoration of the reign of the heart' (MT, 229). The Hermit is not presented in 'the padmasana posture of Buddhist or yogic meditation aiming at the transcendent peace of nirvana, nor is he presented seated on the throne of power making a commanding gesture' (MT, 224). This Hermit is pedestrian, presented to us as walking. His wisdom is won by walking. If we were to say that he 'sauntered', it would be in the original sense of someone on their way to the *sainte terre*, the holy land. He goes around the world as it manifests itself, in all its confusing diversity. He looks for connections, a unity within that multiplicity: the world as multi-coloured, many-splendoured thing. His way is the way of peace, the way of intelligence (which can mean interconnection, *inter-ligare*), the way of harmony, finding unity in diversity. He shows us a pedestrian crossing, combining contemplation and activity. This is the way of the beating heart. Iambic pentameter: the Greek for footbeats of five. 'O, from what power hast thou this powerful might?' Rilke calls it 'heartwork'. We dwell with and in the rhythm of our hearts. The heart is a lonely hunter. It never ceases to breathe. 'It walks day and night and we listen to the steps of its walking' (MT, 226).

THE WHEEL OF FORTUNE

Twenty-two trumps fall into two groups. The journey rolls from the first zero of the Fool to the wider circle of the whole world. The Wheel of Fortune is at the mid-point. It too describes a circle, but one which is of our own making. The machine on this picture is homemade in appearance, not to say makeshift. It describes the endless repetitiveness into which we fall like into a groove once we allow 'fate' to craft our lives, once we are dragged by the pull of whatever forces can control us, from alcoholism to xenophobia in the alphabet of possible addiction. This card describes Fate versus Free Will.

Here we see a pint-sized, ludicrously costumed monster of foreboding appearance, lounging on a platform, wearing a golden crown, and carrying a sword almost as if he has mistaken it for a gun, which he carries on his shoulder as a drunken soldier might when standing to attention. He looks like someone in fancy dress who couldn't quite decide which costume to choose, and ended up wearing bits from each one. The creature is on guard over, but importantly enough, does not supply the movement for, the wheel underneath. There is a dog-like animal descending the wheel and another with rabbit's ears on the ascending rim. These two creatures in helpless tandem provide the motion for the merry-go-round. They have been categorised as the domesticated self entering the depths, and the untamed unconscious emerging into the daylight. Whatever terminology we use, these two prisoners are aspects of ourselves as we lie strapped to the recurring inevitabilities of our repetitively dreary lives. How is it we always get ourselves into exactly the same quicksands every time, whether these be emotional, financial, or workaholic? Life is a treadmill, a conveyor belt, same old routine over and over again, *déjà-vu*.

Our task is to liberate these animal energies that have been, for most of our lives, caught in an instinctual cycle of repetition. The ludicrous little dictator holds them in thrall. The miniature monarch is naked at the same time as wearing a crown: its energy is primal; its power is regal. The costume and body parts are an idol made out of the elements of true worship: what do the monkey-like face, the body and the tail, the bat-like wings remind us of? Who is this charlatan actually aping? Is it not trying to assume an eagle's wings, a bull's body, a lion's tail, and a human face? In other words, aping the eventual revelation of what each one of us could be when that secret is revealed, and our hidden names are called, on the last day of judgement, as the Apocalypse portrays in equally graphic and unusual imagery?

These are all academic questions. The critical point is how do we get off this wheel? What steps do we take to liberate ourselves towards freedom? It is a familiar ploy of the unconscious to distract us, and by 'us' I mean human consciousness striving towards wholeness or completion, by proposing philosophical questions at the very moment when we most need to do something concrete and practical to confront the demands of our instinctual nature, our inner tyrant seated like a porcelain grotesque on the inner wheel of our life.

The Visconti-Sforza deck shows this Wheel of Fortune (see the colour section in this book) in a more explicitly allegorical interpretation. Four human figures are fixed to the wheel. The ascending one says *Regnabo* (I shall reign), and he is growing a pair of ass ears. The figure on top has full-grown ass ears, holds a sceptre and says *Regno* (I reign). The figure on the way down has lost his ass ears and has grown a tail. He says *Regnavi* (I have reigned). The bearded man at the bottom, the only fully human figure of the four, is pictured on his hands and knees. He says *Sum sine regno* (I am without reign). Fortune is enthroned at the centre of the wheel. She is blindfolded and wears a pair of golden wings. This suggests her power and her detached indifference to the human lot. She makes asses of those who, out of hubris, elevate themselves.

The tarot sphinx, as we might call the hominoid ringmaster, presents us with a heroic task, the challenge of human beingness, daring us to find meaning in a system seemingly propelled by mere animal energy. This card at this turning-point in the total journey invites us to break the spell and initiate the painful glory of being human. These animals chained and clothed present a ludicrous travesty of helpless humanity. But the enigmatic sphinx, for all his or her slapstick buffoonery, is actually suggesting the humanisation of animality and the total integration of our humanity, without eradicating any of our earthiness or ejecting any of our necessary apishness.

Animality that has been successfully incorporated becomes the perfect prototype of what the manikin at the top of our card is aping: the Ox, the Lion, the Eagle, Angel/Man. Each of these can be transformed: in the case of the Ox, from impetuous rage to productive concentration, as in the emblem of St Luke; in the case of the Eagle, from being a ferocious bird of prey with an instinct for aggression, to that elevation of heart and spirit which makes it the emblem of St John; in the case of the Lion from being the deadly king of the forest to being the epitome of moral courage, as in the emblem of St Mark; and finally in the case of the angelic man, from showing indifference towards everything, from being that Greek word, a cynic (*kyon* means 'dog'), to becoming the emblem of St Matthew: an angel of objectivity and impartiality. Such metamorphosis exchanges the clumsy structure of the wheel of fortune for that marriage of opposites which is the way of the cross.

The Wheel of Fortune presents us with an 'arcanum', a secret knowledge, a spiritual exercise, a certain know-how. A circle can be a closed circle that turns on itself, a prison, which offers no advancement beyond its circular movement, becoming an eternal repetition of the same. Or it can be turned into an open circle, where each step forward turns it into a spiral. This movement of liberation moves us up a register until we escape from the ring. Such knowledge is based on the belief that above the eternal wheel of repetition, there is God.

The world of the serpent is the world of enfoldment: the serpent biting its own tail is the emblem of this. Earth was once, in the Mesozoic era, a planet of reptiles, and we are descended from these. The Bible tells us that the serpent was more 'cunning' than any of the other creatures on the earth. We have inherited that cunning, which we prefer to call Wisdom. It is a way of aping wisdom, just as the Devil is the ape of God. It is also a kind of intellectual enfoldment; we tend to create for ourselves closed circles. Our brains prefer totality to infinity –

that is the essence of the scientific mentality: to understand the universe in a single formula, if possible. Now the Bible again tells us that we should be as wily as serpents and as simple as doves. The dove is the emblem of release from circular thinking. The dove descends from above and is above the brain and above the head. It leads us upwards, forming a spiral out of the serpent's circle and releasing us from totality into infinity. The dove introduces the reality of spiritual evolution, which allows us as human beings to transcend the otherwise inescapable principle of biological evolution. This is the vicious circle, the wheel of fortune, from birth through growth to death. The dove descending through the air ruptures this circle and opens it to the vertical dimension, the spiral movement of resurrection.

The wheel here presented, if we look at it again, is not an empty circle like the Fool's hollow zero. This wheel's six spokes form the 'I' superimposed on the 'X', which is the Greek monogram for Jesus Christ.

STRENGTH / FORCE

For the first time a mortal woman appears. Fortitude is one of the four cardinal virtues. We are not dealing here with a goddess. Strength or 'Force' is a human being dressed in the fashion of the period. She is a woman of refinement and breeding. No ordinary woman, however, she is taming a lion. She will help him to tame his animal nature so that he will no longer be wholly under its power. This she can do with her bare hands. There are no magic wands or sceptres of power. She explores the dimensions of the beast's need. Her power has the force of 10 cards behind it. 'The force that through the green fuse drives the flower'[1] is strength rather than power. It is not macho might; it is a feminine control, which is not thereby 'effeminate'. 'Only that which does not teach, which does not cry out, which does not persuade, which does not condescend, which does not explain, is irresistible'.[2] This is the strength of nylon rather than of steel. 'The tarot Strength is not afraid. Perhaps by observing her we can get some idea of how best to approach and tame our inner lion. What exactly is the lady doing with her hands? The question has puzzled generations of Tarot commentators. Some say she is closing the lion's mouth. Others see her as opening it. Perhaps the picture is left intentionally ambiguous, for doubtless the woman must perform each action at various times, depending on circumstances. There are times when the instinctual lion needs to yawn and stretch, or rant and rave, or give forth a joyful roar; and there are other occasions when even kings – and especially kings – need to learn patience and restraint' (SN, 205). Strength achieves this end through their mutual involvement.

Tamed by this woman's magic, the beast offers honey freely. She need not kill him to obtain these gifts. The two figures are united in a harmony mirrored in both the design and colours of the card: the golden energy of the lion's strength flows through her arms, radiating through her heart, before leaping to her head where it rests like a golden crown in the centre of her lemniscate hat. She is wearing the Magician's hat, which is easy to recognise. Her number is 1 + 10. In the Roman version XI recalls the Greek monogram in reverse for Christ, which is depicted in the spokes of the wheel in the previous card number 10. Her crown resembles the teeth of an animal. It has transferred power to the crown chakra: her breathing is now an upward movement. The power of the lion's mouth moves upwards.

This role of the feminine as mediating influence between human consciousness and the primitive psyche is present in countless fairy tales, where Beauty and the Beast and The Frog Prince, for instance, tell the same story in different ways. Through a woman's loving acceptance of its bestial nature, the animal is both tamed and transformed. True power is exercised through powerlessness. False power crucifies others and other parts of ourselves. 'The force that drives the water through the rocks/Drives my red blood.' This card is the true force of life.

Sacred Scripture has two Greek words for life: *zoe* and *bios*. The first is life that vivifies; the second is life as inherited. *Bios* passes horizontally from generation to generation. *Zoe* is life from above, vertical connection. The hands of the woman are opening the mouth of the lion upwards, allowing him to breathe vertically. The lion is obedient to the force of its own life, to the profoundest impulse in the depths of its being. *Bios*, as in 'biology', is the horizontal movement of serpent, life as it is passed on from generation to generation. Attaching this horizontal life force to the electrical current of desire produces addictive energy.

Biological processes themselves cause electrical currents and these are generated through chemical decomposition and by the opposition of contrary forces. In other words, such electricity is caused by internal friction in the organism. This alone causes exhaustion and eventually death. Electricity caused by friction in our lives forces us to sleep, death's second self. The heart and our breathing system do not need any sleep. They keep on pumping and inhaling even while we rest; but the remainder of the organism – above all the brain – have to be plunged into a minor death each night, through sleep, having been drained throughout the day by the nervous energy of inner friction. *Bios* thus repairs the damage done by electricity, which is reduced to a minimum during sleep.

A tree, for instance, whose life movement is upwards, is an organism in which the force of *bios* alone prevails. It is thereby almost immortal: trees rarely die, they are nearly always 'killed', whether by storm or chainsaw. Death is simply the price paid for a life lived amidst conflicting opposites. True strength, true power, as displayed in this card, is the energy of resurrected life, which is every second at our disposal. We can choose between life and life, *bios* and *zoe*, ordinary or superabundant life. If we allow the second kind of life to inform our nature, it leads us as from now, to resurrection, life lived to the full and forever. 'I am the resurrection'; 'I have come so that they may have life and have it to the full'; 'Whoever lives and believes in me will never die. Do you believe this?'[3]

THE HANGED MAN

This card represents the reversal of values and aims which should take place during the second half of life, on the second leg of our journey towards maturity. Twelve in Arabic numbers is 1 + 2, which spells the coming together of unity and duality, which in turn gives birth to a third possibility. This third way is always a symbol of renewal and salvation. Here we have taken our life in our hands and are balanced delicately between the shadow at morning striding behind us and that shadow at evening rising to meet us. The tap-root of creativity and of possibility inside us waits like a frightened animal quivering with expectancy.

A young man hangs upside down, tied by one foot to a gibbet, the twin poles of which are truncated trees, each with six bleeding stumps where branches have been lopped off. The trees are growing at either side of a fissure in the earth – a crevice or deep abyss. This puts the young man's head below the earth's surface, buried underground like the roots of both trees. The knob of his head, with its hanging hair, is an underground ball, perhaps a turnip, with the hairy roots characteristic of that vegetable.

Almost instinctively, anyone who sees this card for the first time, itches to turn the Hanged Man right side up. We want to put the head back 'where it belongs'. If you do so, you see the young man quite differently: now, he is delicately poised on one foot and, with arms akimbo, he is really dancing a jig! Viewed from the perspective of the unconscious, he who appeared to be immobilized – held captive – is now freed; he who seemingly had lost balance has now achieved a splendid new equilibrium. Even his face seems to have changed: a scooped out pumpkin at Hallowe'en. He meets our gaze calmly and confidently with a look of authority; he appears to smile as if he knew a secret. He does know a secret: it is the secret of the twelfth major arcana of the tarot.

In order to discover this secret, we must view him again as he first presented himself, dangling helplessly in space. The custom of hanging people in this way was called 'baffling'. The word has travelled down the mysterious paths of language to mean: thwart, frustrate, confuse. The hanged man is enduring a kind of crucifixion. This card is about gravity, about the difference between terrestrial and celestial gravity. In exasperation at intellectual pride, Mother Nature seems to have grasped her impudent son by the heels and shoved his silly brains into the bosom of her earth. According to Mercia Eliade: 'The Taoist, imitating animals and vegetables, hangs himself upside down, causing the essence of his sperm to flow up to his brain. The tan-t'ien, the famous fields of cinnabar, are to be found in the most secret recesses of the brain and belly; there it is that the embryo of immortality is alchemically prepared.'[1] Such 'humility' – being plunged into the earth (humus, in Latin means earth), is a shortcut to reality. A challenge rather than a punishment, Jung says: 'For the unconscious always tries to produce an impossible situation in order to force the individual to bring out his very best. Otherwise one stops short of one's best, one is not complete, one does not realise oneself. What is needed is an impossible situation where one has to renounce one's own will and one's own wit and do nothing but trust to the impersonal power of growth and development.'[2]

After experiencing the new release of energy suggested by the previous card, the hero must have been shocked and dazed by this sudden reversal. He must have felt deeply wronged, impatient to be righted – to be able once more to hold his head high and set his two feet firmly on the path of his quest. He must have suffered long before attaining the degree of acceptance, of almost graceful repose pictured here (SN, 215–25).

He has followed the path of obedience, listening to the words of wisdom which sometimes lead us in directions and to places we would rather not go. In the Christian Gospels we meet this kind of wisdom, which is the opposite of science as we learn it in school. 'Come and see' is the answer given by Christ to those who want to know where he lives, where he finds the source of his magnetic personality. The order is reversed. You come first and then you see. In the wisdom of science you have to see first before you go. This young man acted before he thought about it, his head followed his feet. His feet had reasons for moving that his head had not yet endorsed. His 'will' is party to truths that, as yet, his head, his thinking, does not know. This is the way the future can be mapped out by the divine architect – if he can find a willing spy to reconnoitre the promised land, the land full of promise. Celestial designs for the future can work through such impulse. Here is a man of the future, as we say. He acts first ... as though he knew. Abraham was such a blind father of a stranger future than any had ever foreseen. Suspended between the potential and the real, his will maintains the contact. The gift of reckless availability drawn from some glimmer in the night, subdued brightness beyond the human eye's scale of natural visibility, which allows the precursor to inch a way forward. Darkness of knowledge that goes beyond natural human cognitive powers. Infused radiance. 'The will receives the divine imprint that the head at some time will understand – or not' (MT, 319).

Symbolism is the only means of allowing thought and imagination to keep up, to keep abreast of what the heart and the will are imposing on the whole person. This is where something like the tarot cards can help to assuage the mind, through the diplomacy of imagination, when the will submits to revelation from above. They enable the suspended intellect to get a look in and give it enough glimpses of what might be happening to unite with it in a total act of receptive obedience.

The two trees, between which the Hanged Man is balanced, bear twelve scars where branches have been cut. The Hanged Man is dangling beyond their action and influence. He has released himself into the space, the detached zone, where he can become channel for the future, instrument for the new music, the unheard melodies that are sweeter than any already in our repertoire. The hanging reminds us of crucifixion. Resurrection, which is the goal of the tarot wisdom, is crucifixion that has reached the stage of fructification. It is realised crucifixion (MT, 390). In other words, resurrection is crucifixion which has born fruit. We who come after the crucified one can be like the fig tree: we do not have to blossom; we can grow directly into fruit. The lopped off branches of the trees around the hanged man, crucified like Peter upside down, show the cutting away of grasping fingers and tendrils that leave a space around us, a space of freedom, into which we can extend and expand. Such upheaval is the ferment of our germination, the burgeoning in us of 'shoots of everlastingness', the implantation of that glory which is resurrected life, and which is made visible in the upturned face.

DEATH

Card number thirteen is the only one of the Marseilles deck without a title. Where the name is written on other cards there is a black band with two heads, one male, one female, separated by a red scythe. We have separated life from death in such a way that every sign of this ominous presence has been removed. We have sanitised our mortuaries and beautified our corpses, eliminated the very smell of decay. So that death jumps out at us from dark places unexpectedly. And yet this card is what we are destined to become. At the end of everything we find a skeleton.

After the initial shock when we get this card for the first time, we pull ourselves together and recognise something overly carnivalesque about it. It represents a skeleton with a red bladed scythe standing on blackened earth; the grass is blue against a white horizon where all else has been obliterated. Scattered as harvest of this scythe are two feet, two hands, a pair of dismembered bones, the crowned head of a man, and a woman's head being crushed underfoot by the rather small but elegant foot of the skeleton. We're in the world of comic strips and caricature. The card is not death as a literal reality. It is the scattering, the dissolution of any world of our own. It represents the inevitable termination, the brutal cutting off, or away, which must precede any radical new beginning in our lives. Every eye in the card looks leftwards, towards the west, towards sunset, towards the dark. Death means parting, letting go, the end. It also prepares the way for the new. All sorts of new growth with somewhat fantastic colouring are pushing through the dark loam of the reaper's patch.

And the red colour of the blade suggests that these are emotional ties we need to be trimming ruthlessly. Any progress requires pruning, and each of us is victim to a number of relationships that are holding us down like Gulliver in Lilliput. We need to send the crazy-makers packing, those whose only interest is to be wreckers of our homemade shelters, the makeshift chalets of our lives. Every relationship grows in a greenhouse where tiny fragile plants survive. It is not possible to share this space with those who fling rocks through the framework.

At this point in our journey the fool in us needs to be rescued. He or she is likely to have become Prince Myshkin in Dostoievsky's novel, *The Idiot*. This kind of fool is full of that endless compassion which makes him fall in love with those who are always drowning. His dizzying vertigo is toppling towards the abyss. His so-called love for others is destruction of himself, a kind of selflessness that is even more damning than the most egotistical selfishness. It is time to learn the lesson from the previous card and move forward towards the next one, which is Temperance. Unless we find the balance between love of our own being and love of others, we are dead bodies being dragged around the walls of Troy, where Helen awaits another city she can burn.

Depicted in this card very graphically is the column of the skeleton's spine. It is an X-ray photograph of the backbone we need to develop if we are to live our own lives at the new rhythm of death and resurrection rather than as spineless amphibians who crawl horizontally along the trail strewn with bait by others.

Linking this card with the previous one, we are witnessing a dismemberment. Every aspect of the past life of the one who strives for completion has been dethroned and scattered. The ideas in that head (and the head wears a crown not dissimilar to the one we started out with, in the Chariot) have been dumped unceremoniously. Particular standpoints have been cut from under you: witness your scattered feet. The previous work of your hands is no longer possible since both these hands have been amputated. There is no return to your previous way of being.

Death has provided so many manifestations in our lives: forgetting is a kind of death, as is sleep. These degrees of death reduce us to the level of animals in the first instance, to the level of vegetation in the second, before we are reduced to the mineral level, the skeleton depicted here, in the final degree. When I forget, I am a cow. When I sleep, I am a tree. When I die, I become a rock.

Sleep and oblivion are deaths as preliminary manifestations, minor deaths that are necessary for growth in life. Such growth is exemplified in three realities experienced on a daily basis: remembering, awakening and giving birth. We can make ourselves more conscious of these experiences from the inside as vital preparation for the capital D of death as the final end of life for every one of us, also on a daily basis. In three hundred years from now no one presently inhabiting the world will still be there. We don't need cards to make this ominous prediction. It is a prophecy of which we can be absolutely sure. We will be wiped out, all six billion of us.

The card is a useful reminder, an invitation to build for ourselves, like the ancient Vikings, a ship of death. We can adapt ourselves to this inevitable eventuality by a number of body building exercises. There are, for instance, two kinds of breathing: horizontal respiration, which creates the aeration between the outside and the inside; and vertical breathing, along the column of the spine which causes the airflow between above and below. Singing is more or less the vertical breathing as best accomplished here on earth. Death in its terminal stage effects an abrupt passage from horizontal to vertical respiration. To those who have learnt vertical respiration all through their lifetime and have exercised their bodies in such breathing techniques, death will be a negotiable arc rather than an abrupt angular jerk – an emergence rather than an emergency. Such respiration is what St Paul calls 'freedom in God'. It is a new way of breathing. 'This breathing of the air is an ability. By a divine breath-like infusion, the Holy Spirit makes the soul capable of breathing God in the same circulation of love that the Father breathes in the Son and the Son in the Father. We must not think it impossible that the soul is capable of so sublime an activity as this breathing in God.'[1] In the inhalation of such a breath, death itself is breathing one's last in love. Death comes in the end as the kiss of the eternal one.

XIIII

TEMPÉRANCE

XIIII

TEMPERANCE

Temperance comes from the same word as time. We are learning to juggle time and eternity. The river flows between two containers, one red the other blue: blood and water. The dancing figure of the angel doesn't have to look to see what she is doing. She pours so fluently she doesn't spill a drop. The liquid that flows between the two has no colour. The suggestion is pure energy, which from now on in this journey has to be evenly distributed between both halves of our total self, whether this be spiritual and fleshly, masculine and feminine, conscious and unconscious. More importantly, the energy that she distributes so deftly between the two quite narrow-necked jugs is 'electrical' energy and 'vital' energy. Hers is that unity of being: embodiment of the flow between life and life. Life of flesh and blood, life of the spirit.

Moderation is the Golden Mean between too much and too little. Harmony, balance, peace of mind. We can trust this messenger. She has a five-petalled flower on her forehead in the place where the third eye of supreme consciousness is situated. The flowering of the crown chakra fulfils the flow of all the others up and down like rivers through the tresses of her hair. Earth and growth and human being achieve balance and identity in this movement and this flow. And yet we recognise that she is from another world. Her wings betoken angelhood. She is called the Angel of time, the meeting and blending of opposites. Angels are messengers from God, they tell us of the deepest levels of our unconscious being, they show us the way towards wholeness. The Arabic form of this number 14 combines unity and plurality: the 1 combines with the 4 corners of the world, the 4 elements, the 4 aspects of personality, to produce the 5, the pentagon, which symbolises organic growth and reconciliation of many parts into a greater whole.

We temper justice with mercy; we temper steel to make it strong but also pliable; we temper asceticism to make it compassionate, duty with a sense of humour. Although a heavenly being, Temperance is more human than Justice, for instance. Although she has wings, she stands firmly on the earth we recognise. She is the only winged card of the tarot we meet at our own level, in the foreground, out in the open of the solid earth. Her wings are sketches of our future in store. The evolutionary appetite and osmosis which carried us from having fins and tentacles, to more effective paws and claws, and eventually to our present arms and hands: all of these are results of our being required to touch things which were further removed from ourselves, to extend the sense of touch beyond what we could crush inside our clenched fist. These active extensions of our will to touch are produced through the power of that will and the dream of what that will could reach. The demands of resurrection are such that we are going to have to develop organs of touch that take us very much further than any of the aforementioned tools of touch. Our arms are an expression of our will to be so armed. Wings too are organs that must sprout if the evolutionary appetite is to achieve the dream of angelhood. Celestial gravitation requires some organ that can temper the inexorability of earthly gravitation. We have to devise the means and the will to achieve whatever can release us from such gravitation. Such is the message of the Angel of time.

Human hubris can only create wings of wax like those of Icarus, or wings like bats to fly towards evil. The legitimate wings in our human unconscious allow us to achieve an upward movement, a verticality, a walking with God which means a constant orientation of consciousness towards God. This is the flow between two vases, two currents of energy; it is the law of inspiration. It is thinking together between the human and the divine plane. There are two vases, yours and another's. In order to 'think together' one thing is necessary: humility. I have to bow before an intelligence surpassing mine. I have to yield the author's exclusive copyright to the anonymous co-thinker [MT 393].

Inspiration of the kind being illustrated here means a kind of artistry both active and passive. The Greek language had a middle voice. We have lost both the grammar and the practice. For us everything is either active or passive. I kick you, or I am kicked by you – there is no in-between. Either I compose this piece or somebody else composes it. Inspiration is more than 'I think', or 'I compose'. It is better expressed by 'it thinks' or 'thinking happens'. Even the word 'compose' comes from the Latin *cum* meaning 'with' and *pono*, meaning to 'place' or to 'pitch'. It implies acting with someone else. Two sources, two simultaneous currents mingle and unite wherever you have authentic inspiration of this second kind. No one can teach us the techniques required. You cannot teach inspired art. You submit to it and it teaches you.

XV

THE DEVIL

This card forms another circle: a lower case 'o'. The circle is formed by the ropes hanging loosely around the necks of the male and female creatures who are captives of the cross-eyed hermaphrodite devil. The dark angel is featured with penis, breasts and claws, and looks like a pantomime villain wearing bats' wings and a flower-pot hat. The circle of the noose continues along the sword in his/her left hand, disappears into the blue wing and continues through the antlers, which frame the potlike crown. This devil is potbound, and the vessel on which it stands is chained to the necks of the two who have invented it. Their hands are tied and the only apparent growth in the world around them is what comes out of their heads. A prison wall encloses them. All the rest has been blanked out. Their feet are enmired in black. They are, however, willing prisoners of their own infatuation. The male homunculus looks at the female in a tortured way; she stares blankly ahead. Hell is what you make it. This card is a parody of that other circle, card number XXI, the World; same shape, same size, but entirely peopled by ourselves: a world of our own invention, a vicious circle. This is the world as selfishness – each one of us as slave to every other potential enemy, competitor, rival, withholder. The two in the foreground imagine that they are the hero and the heroine of this play. They fail to see that the drama is taking place in the limelight behind their backs. The secret of this card is simple: as long as we refuse to turn around and confront our inner devil we are not yet human.[1] We can be the most 'perfect' facsimiles, the award-winning, unanimously elected persons of the year, but this façade is the most dangerous of all. Our consciousness is only a surface *avant-garde*. Behind it are the real issues: unconscious prejudices, complexes, weaknesses, neuroses. Any psychic function which is disconnected and works without reference to the total picture of who we are, is devilish. Demons are mostly psychological complexes that have a cancerous effect on the psyche they inhabit.

The number of the card is XV, which becomes 15 in the Arabic version. This combination of digits when added together gives you six, which is the card of The Lovers. The Devil is mostly about love gone wrong. The Apocalypse describes the Devil as Satan: he who stands before the throne of God day and night accusing us. But his other name is Lucifer, the bringer of light. He is that other side of our psyche, which we need to exhume if we are to come to terms with who we are. You don't become enlightened by imitating exemplars of brightness, so-called saints and apostles of light; we only enlighten ourselves by making the darkness conscious.[2] To distance ourselves from this dark possibility within – the fact that we are all potential criminals – we have created a monster to act a main part in the pantomime we prefer to the real drama of our lives: Satan as supernatural sadist or infernal demon. In this guise, the evil that is the shadow side of everything that is bright and good remains hidden to ourselves. This is the devil as scapegoat.

However dangerous at an individual level, this projection becomes lethal at a collective level. The twentieth century was both victim and proof of such blindness. The great plagues of that century, equivalent to the Black Death and other physical plagues of medieval times, were ideological. Ideology is intoxication as opposed to inspiration. It sows the wind and reaps the whirlwind. It is will-power and imagination gone wild. Far from the inspiration of Temperance, which was the last card, this satanic megalomania bases itself on genuine need and real experience, but then it creates from this an outsized monster that sets out to reinvent the whole universe. Any large community, says Jung, composed of wholly admirable persons who have failed to identify their inevitable allegiance to humanity's black collective shadow, is about as intelligent and as moral as 'an unwieldy stupid and violent animal'.[3] Individuals who refuse to confront their inner devils wreak havoc on those around them; whole societies in a similar purblindness unleash pandemonium (a word invented by Milton to describe the chaos of hell). 'The history of the human race supplies us with numerous examples of the transformation of the initial inspiration of temperance into the subsequent intoxication generating demons' (MT, 411).

Hell is our own invention. There is nothing good or bad but thinking makes it so. We are the creators of heaven and hell and there are no demons apart from our own folly. Marx and Engels were originally inspired by that same care for the rights and well-being of the poor which is the hallmark of most religions, whether Buddhist, Christian, Islamic, or Jewish, but the end results of their creation was a work of intoxication, exaggeration, grandiosity, excess. The Nazi regime in Germany is perhaps the supreme exemplar of such satanic dominion. However, every inspired movement can be victim to such devilish deviation. How the teaching of Jesus Christ could have produced the Inquisition is a sobering corrective to any vilification or self-righteousness on the part of Western Europeans.

The corollary to this capacity to endorse satanic regimes is the corresponding propensity to denounce them as diabolical. Paranoia about the alphabet of evil simply spells failure to face the fact that no one of us stands outside the collective dark shadow of humanity. Albigensians, Bolshevists, CIA, Drug Barons, Extra-Terrestrials, Freemasons, Greens, Hotentots, Indians, Jews, KGB, Lefties, Marxists, neo-Nazis, OPEC, Paratroopers, Queers, Revolutionaries, Saracens, Taliban, UFOs, Vivisectionists, Witches, Xenophobes, Yankees, Zionists. These are samples of the many labels we can create for every letter of the alphabet, projecting onto others internal bile we have accumulated, which we need to launch towards some spittoon to distance ourselves from the enemy and identify a fall-guy. But it's a frame-up, which catches us on our own security camera: each one of these caricatures is a mugshot of our own inner demon, the Mr Hyde to our Dr Jekyll. We have provided a sketch of the enemy within, the very one we have been avoiding all our lives. The hissing misnomer, scud-missile released by our own panic button, is more descriptive of the discharger than the designated target.

The two figures in the foreground of this card are essentially smug and self-satisfied. To release them from their enslaved lives something akin to the lightning flash and the thunderbolt of the next card may be necessary.

XVI

THE TOWER

Here is a tall slender tower. The top, looking somewhat like a crown, has been struck by lightning, dislodged and falling. The lightning itself looks like a featherduster with tongues of fire licking through leaves of gold. It is not very threatening or overwhelming. But it is effective. The tall tower is destroyed. We notice that it has no door. Three windows of uneven size are placed in the higher storeys. Two male figures falling from the tower are upside down as they reach the ground. They don't look disconsolate. Rather with both hands reaching outwards they seem to be almost grateful for contact with the earth. Spherical balls of fire surround the picture, giving the impression of global disturbance. The title of the card in French is *La Maison Dieu* (God's house). This could have been a mistaken rendering of *Maison de feu* (house of fire); or, if the original was Italian, it could have been a misspelling of *Caso* (meaning 'fate') for *Casa* (meaning 'house'). If we build a tower of Babel it carries within the seeds of its own destruction.

The card is also about God's houses, whether temples, churches, synagogues, or mosques, and the principle expressed in the ancient psalm: *nisi dominus aedificaverit domum, in vanum laboraverunt qui aedificant eam* (Unless the Lord builds the house, in vain do its builders labour). Two people are being liberated from enforced incarceration. Some tarot packs call this card 'the stroke of liberation', referring to the lightning that knocks off the top. 'Stroke' is ambiguous: it can be with a cane – like the Zen master's – or it can be a caress. It is a bolt out of the blue, a lightning flash, a symbol of Divine energy. Birth and death are obviously the major shocks. This one is a display of naked power. It comes immediately from heaven and is not mediated through either a magician's wand, an emperor's sceptre, or a pope's crosier. The Holy Spirit has been described as such fire from heaven.

Asklepios, for instance (who later became the God of medicine), was slain by Zeus' thunderbolt. Plutarch saw lightning as the originator of all life. The symbolism is heavily phallic. The beginning is envisaged as primal waters fertilised by primitive energy. Contemporary science conjectures that such might be the case for life on earth. We could all have been sparked off by lightning. In this picture the lightning is not directed at the people; it is directed at the tower itself.

The tower itself is like a hard outer shell, a nut which, when cracked open, lets fall two living kernels; these might even be two parts of the same person. The two people are falling to the earth and reaching for green-leaved plants from which, through which, they seek revivification. They don't look unhappy or as if they are being evicted from their home.

Listen to Tomberg writing in the 1960s: 'The 16th Major Arcanum of the Tarot is a warning addressed to all authors of systems, where an important role is assigned to a mechanical ingredient. Our principal danger (if not the only true danger) is that of preferring the role of builders of the tower of Babel (no matter whether personally or in a community) to watching over "as gardeners or vine-growers the garden or the vine of the Lord" ... confusing the tower with the tree, recruiting masons instead of gardeners' (MT, 459–60).

The dictator and the magnate both need equally the liberating thunderbolt from above to return to the way of purely human evolution. Wisdom is a tree, not a tower. It is the tree of death and resurrection, the tree of the Cross. Mythologically this tree grew from seeds that Adam took with him from the Garden of Eden, so it is also the tree of knowledge and of life. From it grows the good news of resurrection, that great alchemical operation of the successful transmutation of the human being. In practical wisdom, as is required by resurrection of the body, and as encoded in the tarot cards, there is nothing mechanical or surgical. You will not find any devices in it, no recipes, no programmes, no quick-fix solutions, whether mental, ceremonial or physical. No exercises, no meditation techniques that would allow us to go beyond ourselves and reach paranormal states of being. You will not find, for example, a technical method of awakening the 'lotus centres' by pronouncing mantric syllables accompanied by especially taught breathing practices designed for this end.

The way of the tarot means cordiality which warms the heart. This way is not about ready-made answers to every question: well-being obtained by minimum effort with maximum results. Its questions are crises that every human being meets on the road of life, and the 'answers' it elicits are states of consciousness that result from these crises.

What is being proposed is an art of becoming. The symbols that the tarot uses are 'ferments' or 'enzymes' of thought, whose troubling presence disquiets ordinary patterns of thinking. If it were a 'system' of philosophy, an intellectual instrument, it would have died long ago. It is instead a way of genuinely experiencing the breath of the living spirit (MT, 453).

The marriage of opposites and not their divorce is the basis of such wisdom. We are not talking about mushy compromise. We are offering the sign of the cross and the magic of the cross, which promises that all shall be well and nothing lost. Divorce between the two opposite sides would be a catastrophe. We reject the surgical principle of divorce and war. All can and should be saved. Our faults and our vices are not monsters, they are lost sheep that must be brought back to the flock: symbol of the soul's choral harmony. This card reveals 'to serious meditation the comprehensive arcanum of the relationship between will and destiny – between what one wants and what happens' (MT, 443). 'It teaches a general and universal law, that is a law which operates both on a small scale and on a grand scale, in individual biography as well as in that of mankind, and in the past, present and future equally. According to this law, he who rebels against this "higher self" will no longer live under the law of the vertical but rather under that of the horizontal, he will be "a fugitive and a wanderer on earth" (Genesis, 4:12)' (MT 450).

This meditation on the card of the Tower has been taken in large part from Valentin Tomberg, who was writing in the 1960s. My own views on this arcanum will appear in the last chapter, when analysing the destruction of the Twin Towers as a symptomatic event of the twenty-first century. Tomberg's commentary is all the more striking in light of this contemporary picture of the card.

THE STAR

In the star we meet for the first time a naked human being, stripped of officialdom and social trappings. Yet this is vulnerable humanity; there are no wings involved. The four elements of nature are also here together for the first time: earth, air, fire, water. These can also represent the four essential psychic functions: thinking, feeling, intuition, sensation. The woman kneels and pours from two jugs. This action relates her visually to the card of Temperance. However, whereas Temperance was pouring white liquid from a blue container into a red one, both the Star's containers are red. They contain full-blooded humanity – physical and bodily human feeling.

Above the kneeling figure, seven coloured stars revolve around a central double star. This last is a yellow eight-pointed star superimposed upon a similarly eight-pointed red one. Black lines connect the yellow star's eight points to a centre where they converge like the spokes of a wheel. All these stars are on a white background.

The kneeling figure is a hidden aspect of our inner being, held prisoner and refused suffrage in the all-male society depicted in the tower. The stars shine as a result of the dethronement and eviction accomplished in that previous card. The two green trees in the background, with a blackbird perched on one, remind us of the Tree of Knowledge and the Tree of Life in the Garden of Eden. This was before we began to build the tower of Babel. And the blackbird could be the one sent by Noah out of the ark to see if there was dry land after that universe had been drowned in the flood. The girl's two red jugs are pouring two blue streams of water, one into the river and the other onto the land. This is the brave new world that Shakespeare told us of in *The Tempest*. The Tempest that cracked open the Tower shook out unconsciously the wonder of the people who were in it. And here in this neighbouring card is

Miranda, again full of wonder, watering the newly fashioned earth.

The card has been associated with Baptism, which also generates a new creation. 'In the beginning God created the heavens and the earth. Now the earth was a formless void, there was darkness over the deep, and God's spirit hovered over the water' (Genesis 1:1). 'God said, "Let there be a vault in the waters to divide the waters in two." And so it was. God made the vault, and it divided the waters above the vault from the waters under the vault. God called the vault "heaven"... God said "Let there be lights in the vault of heaven" ... and so it was.' (Gen. 1:9–16). These lamps were stars.

After the Tower as the Arcanum of human building programmes and massive construction, we reach the Star which is the arcanum of the true scale, ratio and proportion of human growth. This is a different kind of space to the one envisaged by the Tower, and a different kind of time to that being spun on the Wheel of Fortune. The eight stars are openings to the heavens above. The enlarged one is the eighth day, when morning came and evening passed into eternity. It is the sabbath day when the Lord God rested and the creatures of the earth rested with God. The perfection of this awning was riveted to eternity by the cross of Christ, which forms the centre-piece in black lines on the two superimposed stars. The stars are also what we call the Milky Way. They are the heavenly breasts through which the milk of eternity can suckle the vulnerability of earth.

Two streams of water, representing consciousness and the unconscious dimension of that vulnerable humanity, are poured from hands which are open outward. Hands that no longer hoard what they do not need, or build beyond themselves.

One of the ancient Hebrew psalms describes such trees growing beside the flowing water: 'The righteous flourish like the palm tree, and grow like a Lebanon cedar ... still bearing fruit when they are old, still full of sap, still green.'

A tower is built; a tree grows. This is the difference between the two cards. The two processes have much in common: an increase in volume and a movement upwards. However, the tower is dry and dessicated height; the tree oozes with free-flowing sap from the root, through each layer of the trunk, right up to the topmost branches. The sap is what makes it grow.

> O chestnut tree, great-rooted blossomer,
> Are you the leaf, the blossom or the bole?[1]

The difference between natural growth and urban expansion is that growth flows through the organism, whereas building programmes sprawl without inner vitality. The sky for them is the limit only because they have never understood the organic nature of proportionality.

The theme of this seventeenth arcanum of the tarot is the universal sap of life, the phenomenon of natural and human growth as opposed to gargantuan development out of all proportion to the shape of the environment. It is water which makes it possible for shrubs to grow in the sandy desert; it is the woman pouring the water who tends such growth and is its guardian; finally, it is the stars, from which the light emanates and is transformed into fluidity through the woman as intermediary. The witnesses and the wherewithal of such growth are water, spirit and blood. These are the gauges of graceful symmetry.

This card is about the way an acorn becomes an oak or a crying child becomes an adult. There is an inner sap that ties the end product to the original embryo. There is a proportionality, a recognisable strain which identifies the one as issuing from the other. Building construction understands no such natural constraint. Its only law is expansion to the utmost bounds of the earth; its only limit is the cliff-edge.

Growth is in two directions at the same time. It happens through the spiral, not the closed circle or the wheel. These only force us to turn in circles. 'Both spiritual and biological growth are outwards and upwards at the same time. The so-called "tree-ring" circles, which are formed each year between the bark and the centre of the trunk of the tree, are the proof and the result of such circular growth in two dimensions – vertical and horizontal – at the same time, i.e. proceeding in a spiral' (MT, 483).

The spiral is the action of the sap within. This card shows us the relationship between stellar, female, and fluidic principles of growth. There are stars in the sky, there is a naked

woman pouring water from two vases, and shrubs are growing.
The spiral of growth descends from the stars, to the woman, to
the water, to the shrubs. The card answers the question: What
does a tree need to live? Water and the feminine, earth and
stars. So says the seventeenth card of the major arcana of the
tarot. Our growth must be rounded and upward, organic and
proportional. It cannot be purely vertical, nor can it remain
horizontal. In between these two directions, the way to avoid
eternal repetition of the same is represented by the spiral, what
Yeats called 'perne in a gyre':

> O sages standing in God's holy fire
> As in the gold mosaic of a wall,
> Come from the holy fire, perne in a gyre,
> And be the singing-masters of my soul.[2]

THE MOON

The journey through the night started after the Hermit with the double-digit cards. The Moon describes us emerging from the watery depths and returning towards the light. In itself the Moon card means darkness, night, and the deep exploration of inner spaces. We are moving towards the dawn on paths that are hardly lit and difficult to make out. All our human talents and faculties are rendered useless, our senses can no longer function; we are thrown back on the tiny beam of inner light which helps us forward.

It takes a long time to prepare for this transition. Confronted with this card for the first time, nearly everyone has difficulty finding a way in. There are no human figures. You can't empathise with any of the creatures here. The golden towers are enticing, but there does not seem to be a way across the water.

This is lunar land, the realms of the night where the ego has no authority and must abdicate in favour of powers that it cannot comprehend. One is thrown back on the primitive wisdom of the body.

The card describes the journey to/through the unconscious. Such a place is not to be lingered in. It is because we Western Europeans have so neglected it that this side of ourselves must now be emphasised. Jung says that both parts must be balanced. 'If our psychology is forced to stress the importance of the unconscious, that does not in any way diminish the importance of the conscious mind. It is merely the one-sided over-evaluation of the latter that has to be checked by a certain relativisation of values. But this relativisation should not be carried so far that the ego is completely fascinated and overpowered by the archetypal truths. The ego lives in space and time and must adapt itself to their laws if it is to exist at all.'[1]

The water is similar to the pool in the previous card. The crayfish (which moves backwards when swimming) seems to be reaching towards the opposite shore. This creature represents an early manifestation of the evolutionary process and the stages of conscious unfolding; a shell-fish, like all of us, seeking to rise out of the water and the slime. However, it is also ambivalent, like us. Its claws are outstretched as if reaching towards the Eternal City, yet they remain claws, and its habitual armour is present and correct, resisting change.

The coloured drops are falling upwards. Far from raining down dew from above, they seem to be draining the earth from below. A swamp is followed by a desert. This is the arcanum of the inseparable couple – the earth and its satellite, the moon. It pictures the relationship between them. At some point in our lives each of us has to walk on the moon. It is a small step for each human being but a huge step for our humanity. At the beginning of this process, intelligence and unconscious wisdom have so little in common that communication between them is reduced almost entirely to dreams, that state of consciousness where intelligence, although present, is most passive. But soon this communication is extended to the waking state also. The language of communication then becomes the language of symbols, including those of the tarot cards.

There are two animals baying at the moon on the far side of the water on the pathway that leads between the two towers. These have been depicted as a dog and a wolf. To descend into the depths means to be deprived of one's usual daytime companions. However, as 'man's best friend', the dog represents all our instinctive wisdom in a form sympathetic to us. The wolf, on the other hand, stands for that other side of our nature that is untamed and vicious. Our path lies between these two instinctual drives – the howling wolf and the faithful dog. Yet the whole of our instinctual nature must be validated. We have to acknowledge and approach, befriend and harness, all aspects of the person we really are. Otherwise there is no possible progress from the underground pool where we emerge as invertebrate mammals, through the desert where we learn to assume our animal nature, to the golden towers of our ultimate destination as children of eternity.

There are two kinds of people: sun people and moon people. The first are hail and hearty, they live outdoors and thrive on sport; they enjoy life with no thought for its other side, which is death. Not just death as an end but death as rust or mould which corrodes every moment from the day we are born. To be completely a sun person is to be careless, almost alive as an animal is alive. Life and death have to achieve a balance in our mood swings. We have to spend some time on the dark side of the moon. The blending of the two is what creates in us a depth of humanity. Esau and Jacob in the Bible are sun and moon men, according to Thomas Mann. Jacob's son Joseph achieved the balance that comes from dwelling for a time in the lunar underworld: 'For sympathy is a meeting of life and death; true sympathy exists only where the feeling for the one balances the feeling for the other. Feeling for death by itself makes for rigidity and gloom, a feeling only for life by itself, for flat mediocrity and dull-wittedness. Wit and sympathy can arise only where veneration for death is moderated, and has, so to speak, the chill taken off by friendliness to life; while life, on the other hand, acquires depth and poignancy. This happened in Joseph's case; and his shrewd and friendly temper was the result.'[2] But it does not do to remain in the underworld under the lunar spell for too long. The Virgin moon does not give itself to any one. The essence of moonlight is reflection. The earthlings who walked on the moon's surface found little, but they brought back a beautiful photograph of the earth they had left behind – look there, the moon seemed to be telling them, your own earth is where you will find what you seek!

Lot's wife turned into a pillar of salt because she looked back; she lingered too long in the valley of death. 'The laws of the underworld are strict: anyone who eats there, even if this is just one seed of pomegranate, is not permitted to return to the upper world. What happened to the kidnapped Persephone? Whoever sits down in Hades one single time, even if this is just for a brief moment, will sit forever like Theseus and Perithoos on the footstools of forgetting, from which they will never again rise. All of this makes it clear that the descent into the underworld is a task that wants to be performed and should not become an end in itself.'[3] Sallie Nichols (SN 313–325) continues the analogy, quoting people who forever attend self-improvement courses: Valuable as these may be when one finds a hard core of participants in these groups who move continuously from one group to the next, these people no longer want to return to everyday life. They have forgotten what they actually wanted, why they originally set out. So the moon journey has to be undertaken, but it must not be used for self-beautification, nor should it be exploited. You don't explore the secrets of your own inner geography out of curiosity or boredom: using the unconscious for such purposes is dangerous and destructive. Exploitation of our inner nature is as detrimental to us and to it as it has been for the outer nature of our planet. The next generation will have to pay the price.

LE · MAT

Zero   The Fool
Ancien Tarot de Marseille

I The Magician
Ancien Tarot de Marseille

II   The High Priestess
Ancien Tarot de Marseille

III   The Empress
Ancien Tarot de Marseille

IIII   The Emperor
Ancien Tarot de Marseille

V   The Pope
Ancien Tarot de Marseille

VI   The Lover
Ancien Tarot de Marseille

VII   The Chariot
Ancien Tarot de Marseille

VIII Justice
Ancien Tarot de Marseille

VIIII The Hermit
Ancien Tarot de Marseille

X   The Wheel of Fortune
Ancien Tarot de Marseille

XI   Strength / Force
Ancien Tarot de Marseille

XII   The Hanged Man
Ancien Tarot de Marseille

XIII   Death
Ancien Tarot de Marseille

XIIII Temperance
Ancien Tarot de Marseille

XV   The Devil
Ancien Tarot de Marseille

XVI   The Tower
Ancien Tarot de Marseille

XVII   The Star
Ancien Tarot de Marseille

XVIII   The Moon
Ancien Tarot de Marseille

XVIIII   The Sun
Ancien Tarot de Marseille

XX   The Judgement
Ancien Tarot de Marseille

XXI   The World
Ancien Tarot de Marseille

The Wheel of Fortune
Visconti-Sforza deck

The Tower
Lorcan Walshe

THE SUN

The sun looks down on every creature in the world. Its span extends to all the earth. Its rays shine on the good and the bad. It gazes outwards. It does not focus on individual people. In the sweathouse of the world it can warm or it can burn; its rays become drops of sweat or of dew, depending on the climate or the places they infiltrate. The sun is one of the few inescapable influences on planet earth.

Underneath its all-pervading presence on this card it shines its light on two figures who are standing on the earth but who have built a solid wall behind or around them. Good fences seem to have, in this instance, made for good neighbours. These look like brothers. One touches the other with a hand behind his head. The other places an open palm on his brother's heart. This is the major arcana of human cooperation. In the composition of this card the sun with its rays, its influence, occupies three quarters of the space involved. The remainder charts the play-pen of the twins. This is brotherhood as it might have been, as the Gemini constellation of the longest days might have ordained. Cooperation between head and heart, between wisdom and spontaneity. This is the brother and sisterhood that every revolution has sought to achieve: liberty, equality, fraternity. Not the rivalry introduced by Cain and Abel, nor the temperamental estrangement of Jacob and Esau. There are six coloured dewdrops on either side of the twins and one conspicuous blue one uniting their minds in unanimity of spirit. The twelve others represent the zodiacal circle of the stars in the constellation of cosmic mysteries, and the twelve archetypal motivating images identified in the collective unconscious. When these two inner and outer space patterns are aligned, purity of heart and mutual trust can become the ruling principles everywhere under the sun. The sun in this card is designed as such a unifying mandala. At eighty years of age, C. G. Jung describes this as the mid-point, the exponent of all paths, and that all the paths he had been following were leading back to this centre.[1] There is a centre of gravitation which is the heart. Mandalas are cryptograms concerning the state of the self and the state of the world. Teilhard de Chardin saw for this new century of ours 'a vast movement of convergence'. Even the very numbers of human beings populating the planet, combined with the increasing network of communication between each and every one of these, force a change of attitude. We have to get used to a new kind of proximity and learn to live at close quarters.

Here the principle of cooperation must replace the law of the survival of the fittest. It must be true to say that this principle of cooperation, the diurnal principle of Gemini, has played an equally important role in the evolution of humanity as the much vaunted Darwinian theory: the nocturnal principle of the struggle for existence. Whatever the truth may have been in the past, while the human species was struggling for survival on the planet, a new situation has dawned today. With over 6 billion human beings living under the sun, there can no longer be any room for war, or for any kind of strife as the means for survival. The principle of cooperation has put an end to that possibility. Because it was one of the most ingenious inventions of cooperation which allowed the human species to split the atom. 'At the crucial instance when the explosion was about to happen or not to happen, the first artificers of the atomic bomb were crouched on the soil in the desert. When they got to their feet it was over, it was mankind who stood up with them, instilled with a new sense of power.' For the first time in history, Teilhard de Chardin reminds us, hundreds and thousands of trained minds in a period of three years, thanks to unprecedented advances in communications technology, produced a technical accomplishment which might have taken a century of isolated effort: the atomic bomb, which was the result of such intense cooperation, brought about an essential change of plane in the level of human power. With this terrifying breakthrough, whatever truth there may have been in the age-old axiom about war bringing peace had been shattered. From now on self-preservation, conservation, survival could only be achieved through peace. War has been turned into the ultimate enemy and unparallelled threat to survival. 'Everything that formerly made for war now makes for peace, and the zoological laws of conservation and survival must wear an opposite sign if they are to be applied to humankind. The whole phenomenon has been reversed.'[2]

Such reversal and regroupment has been summarised in a cryptic formula by Brendan O'Regan, who has worked all his life towards this new world government by cooperation: MMM WWW means 'Mankind must manage a world without war.' Our choice is as simple as naked brothers and sisters walking together under the sun: we adopt this pattern as our way of being from now on or we annihilate ourselves and the planet on which we walk.

The corollary is featured in the wall behind the two brothers. If we fail to protect the fragile sunglasses which shield us from the overwhelming power and heat of the sun; if we continue to use the resources of the earth in the careless and predatory fashion which has characterised our stewardship to date; if we refuse to conduct ourselves as one species among many whose well-being and health depend upon judicious arrangement and tempered use of the resources available to us all; then nature itself will turn against us and by destroying the equilibrium of our environment we open ourselves to inevitable destruction.

The sun in this card has a human face. Universe as a word means turned towards the one. The focus of our evolutionary appetite as a planet is towards the personalising personality of the universe, which in Christian terms is the *sol justitiae*, the sun of justice, the second person of the Trinity, who has been from the beginning the saviour of the world. It is through our becoming persons united with him and through our dialogue as persons with one another that we shall constitute the communion of persons that this card illustrates. Not just in the persons of the two brothers, but also in the connection between the individual points which make up the periphery of the solar mandala through their meeting as radii in the emerging face at the centre. The edges of this face are etched with lines, each one a depth charge from the surrounding circle of individuated persons.

XX

THE JUDGEMENT

Here the scattered seeds of the thirteenth card, Death, have sprouted into another life. This judgement is final. It is objective as compared with Justice, which was a balance exercised within the realm of virtue in a world constructed by ourselves. Cardinal virtues come from the Latin word hinge, and those four hinges that were attached to our own front door – justice, temperance, fortitude and prudence – must now meet a crisis. The Greek word for judgement is crisis (*krísis*), and the last judgement will be the aim, the meaning, the summary of our whole history. Will we have become what we were meant to have become or will we have fallen short of the mark? There will be no compensatory prizes, no marks awarded for effort: we either *are* what we could have been – resurrected – or we *are* not. There is a distinct division and opposition in the card between higher and lower. The angel with the trumpet is bursting through the space occupied by the sun. The sun of justice rises from a world above the natural sun of our world. The trumpet (coming from the same word as the trump cards, announcing the triumph) is traditionally blown by Gabriel, whose name in Hebrew means 'The power of God'. All angel names end in 'el', which is one word for 'God', as in Elohim. So, Israel, Michael, Gabriel, Raphael, are different manifestations of the divine energy at work in the universe. The banner in the hand of the angel with a cross on a square white surface represents the meeting-place of opposites. It is the crossroads of the four corners of the world, the hub of the universe. *Erexit cornu salutis*. He has raised a horn of salvation. There is a call to resurrection. It is cosmic love which will warm us to resurrected life. The trumpet is almost a suction pump pulling us out of the tomb. Then the mother and the father who gave us biological life turn into god-parents: our heavenly or spiritual mother and father helping us spiritual adolescents towards the pubescence of resurrected life. Judgement is not depicted here as damnation, punishment, divine retribution. This is the liberation of someone from a dark underworld into a great space of light. This is resurrection as liberation from prison, from the confined restrictions of a circumscribed coffin. What is authentic, essential, divine is being freed from an earthly dungeon. Freed from solitary confinement. At either side of that opening, as with our coming into the world, our mother and our father stand aside to let us through. We are sons and daughters of a man and a woman, and it is on this basis that we shall be judged. We shall not judge ourselves; nor shall we be judged by our mother and father. We shall not be judged by Satan, he who stands day and night before the throne of God accusing us. In the end we shall be judged by love. And if your heart condemns, then God is greater than your heart.

All the figures in this card are humanised and in communication with each other – being judged is about whether or not you have become a fully human being. Resurrection is not some all-powerful divine act, but the visible and tangible effect of the meeting and the union of divine love with human being. What is the resurrection of the body? 'Modern science has come to an understanding that matter is only condensed energy. Sooner or later it will discover that "energy" is condensed psychic force and that all psychic force is the "condensation" of consciousness, therefore spirit' (MT, 574).

If our physical body were the product of our spirit alone, it would be the perfect instrument of our spiritual freedom. But because the vertical line of condensation is traversed by the horizontal line of heredity, propagation by birth conflicts with resurrection, such is the cross of human existence. The biological fashions a particular will, which crosses swords with the 'personal' will of our true spirit. Whatever the physical mechanism of heredity may be, it results in the imitation, voluntary or involuntary, of a ready-made model, instinctual conformity to DNA, instead of accomplishment of creative acts. To imitate or to create – this is the choice and the trial, the crisis (or judgement) of every soul in the process of resurrection.

We become a new creation, a new way of being. This requires a kind of breathing, eating, drinking, looking after ourselves, and living on the planet. There are two orders that must be distinguished: the order of creation and the order of sanctification. We are involved, each one of us, with God as creator, in the order of power, and God as lover in the order of vulnerability. God created in order to be gracious. The world is the platform, the stage, on which, in which, through which, the drama of freedom and love can take place. This is the story of grace. Which is God's crisis management, his peace process, his strategy for our salvation, in spite of ourselves and our much-vaunted freedom, his way of seducing us. Grace is the Meccano set that allows us to stand up vertically (with a sacrament for each joint) rather than settle for horizontal lethargy. Sin means in Hebrew and in Greek 'missing the mark': settling for horizontal life rather than vertical life. We crawl rather than stand tall. We were meant to be violins playing exquisite music; we prefer to use the delicate instrument of ourselves for stirring lukewarm porridge. The judgement is about whether we made it as a person or whether we stick to being an individual. We are made of dust and earth, made as vessels of clay, as pots thrown by an almighty potter. The effect of His love on us is to break the potbound periphery and open us out through the cracks. We have to be broken open. The walls have to be razed. We have to be ploughed like earth being prepared for sowing, which is what happened in previous cards. The passion of individualism which is instinctually in our nature as a necessity for self-preservation, self-promotion, self-fulfilment, has to be superseded by the passion of ecstasy, the movement which pours us out into the space between us and other people, accomplishing in us the movement which makes us capable of real love, *Capax Dei*. We are born individuals; we become persons by this expansion of ourselves into the antechamber of the other. We have to do for ourselves what God has already done for himself in our regard: break out of our natural mode of being and ensure that our nature no longer determines the limits of our personhood.

It is not a question of either/or, of choosing this world or the next world, of choosing God or the creation, of being human or being divine. It is a question of all/and. What is being proposed is not exclusion, denial, mortification, destruction of some particular element of what we are now, in order to develop some hybrid variation of ourselves, grafted onto the divine stem at a point above those areas which we intend to bypass or eliminate. The evolution which we must achieve will be a transformation and elevation of the whole human being to a level where the imperatives of biological reproduction will not be as pressing or overpowering, but where the vocation to love will be more specifically human, more personal, more total.

It is a question of becoming fully human. Our whimpering reluctance is understandable in the way that it is understandable not to want to get out of bed in the morning or not to want to get into an aeroplane and fly. Most children regret having to become adults; perhaps caterpillars resent having to push themselves to be butterflies. But the point is this: we were made to be persons and persons in love; anything less than that is diminishment, deprivation, abnegation. The word 'person' was invented by Judaeo-Christianity to cope with the immense reality they were discovering about themselves, because they had been chosen as love objects by God. As the caterpillar moves from chrysalis to butterfly, we too can move from biological life to resurrected life. The latter is accomplished through the power of love, which changes us from individuals into persons. God came on earth to teach these same persons the meaning of the word love. On this we shall be judged.

XXI

LE · MONDE

THE WORLD

With this card we have come full circle. The composition forms a capital 'O' surrounded by a square housing in each of its corners – the four corners of the world – the signs of the four evangelists: The eagle and the angel are above; the lion and the ox are below. Inside the circle a naked woman stands on one foot. If you turn the figure upside down it becomes the figure of the hanged man. In her left hand she holds a scroll, in her right hand a pen. The world is encircled by a wreath of leaves, woven with the blue red and gold colours of the father, the king (gold), the son (red), and the spirit (blue). A blood-red cross forms the intersection of the whole wreath of leaves at the top and at the bottom. The cross on top has points of exit from the circle. The growth of the leaves is downwards on both sides from the cross at the top towards the cross at the bottom. Each of the emblematic creatures wears a halo signifying completion; the halo of the ox is formed by the circle of the world itself.

These four represent the four cardinal virtues, which have matured into prudence, fortitude, justice and temperance. There has been integration of the higher and the lower instincts and faculties. Groups of four in the New Testament include The Four Horsemen of the Apocalypse, the representations of the four evangelists: Matthew, Mark, Luke, and John. The ox for Luke, the eagle for John, the lion for Mark and the man/angel for Matthew. The origin of such animal representation could be Ezekiel I:

> There came the likeness of four living creatures And they had the likeness of a man. And every one had four faces: the face of a man, and the face of a lion, on the right side, the face of an ox on the left side. They four also had the face of an eagle.

The sacred number seven is the four of these virtues, which act as rivets to the three of the Trinity. This card is the sum of three times the sacred seven. The dancing figure in the middle of the circle is humankind as it should always have been in its resurrected state, future perfect paid-up member of the Blessed Trinity.

The star was naked, Miss World is nude. Adam and Eve in the garden saw that they were naked and were ashamed. Those reborn in the *nuditas, paupertas et humilitas Christi*[1] are clothed in glory. It is a way of being human: the way, the truth and the life. The caterpillar becomes a butterfly in an osmosis of resurrection. The nude is the body transfigured. The body does not become a work of art by direct transcription. We are put off by wrinkles, spots, blemishes, bags under the eyes. Nothing is less attractive than a mass of naked figures unadorned. The nude is an architecturally designed representation of the rhythmic proportions of the beauty of the body. It gains its enduring value by reconciling several contrary states. 'It takes the most sensual and immediately interesting object, the human body, and puts it out of reach of time and desire; it takes the most purely rational concept of which mankind is capable, mathematical order, and makes it a delight to the senses.'[2]

This last card is the tarot mandala, the symbol of psychic wholeness. It hatches an eagle's egg guarded at each corner of the squared circle by the same tetramorphs that presided in anarchic fashion over the wheel of fortune in card number ten. The egg contains the world soul from which will emerge the eagle or the phoenix, symbols of the liberated one. The dancer moves at the still point of the turning world, situated at the centre of the quadratic halo. The angel, the eagle, the lion and the ox provide stability and centredness, cardinal virtues, aspects of self, functions of consciousness, riveted corners of the world. 'One only lives while one is dancing,' said one of the world's greatest, Isadora Duncan, when one's feet are moving in time to the rhythm of the universe. Following that beat is forever moving the dancing skeleton and raising the body from the dead. Yeats puts it more rhythmically:

O body swayed to music, O brightening glance
How can we tell the dancer from the dance?

Resurrection is an art form. It is living, acting, doing miraculously, as opposed to 'naturally': it is walking on water, turning water into wine; liberating captives; restoring health; ushering in the kingdom of God. The human machine functions normally according to the determined programme: 'maximum pleasure at minimum cost', says Tomberg. 'To bless those that curse you is a miracle from the point of view of the "normal and natural" functioning of the reactions of the human machine. This does not just happen, it is done (it is created).' It is like an art work – it is a truth that enters the world through human being. 'It is only through the miracle that true being expresses itself, that the creative Word is revealed.' And Tomberg is talking about a kind of 'doing' which is similar to what Heidegger says about 'poetry' as *poiein* ('something done') in Greek: 'One only does miracles, and all that is done is a miracle, and nothing is done without it being a miracle. All that which is not a miracle is not really done – it happens as a part of automatic functioning' (MT, 350).

Such living is a form of love. Doing of this kind comes from the energy of love which we have been given. In ourselves it incarnates as being in perfect and full flow: the centre of our axial equilibrium. Marie-Louise von Franz puts her finger on the pulse of it as she describes the right foot of the dancer in this card: 'A feeling of standing on solid ground inside oneself, on a patch of inner eternity which even physical death cannot touch.'³

Christ came on earth to institute the life of the sacraments, which is the ontological way of transforming our biological existence into resurrected life. This happens by sealing our verticality in seven places in seven different ways, to allow us to stand upright. It can also achieve this through a symbolic community of seven, each one being more characteristically (the origin of the word 'character', *sphragis*, is the Greek word for the 'seal') an embodiment of each of these seals or chakras. We are talking about the kind of love that moves mountains, that works miracles, that allows a mother to lift a lorry off her child being crushed, that pushes the human body to the limits of performance and beyond.

Baptism gives access to the love life of the Trinity. It connects us umbilically to Christ as the true vine and penetrates our spinal column at the muladhara chakra (*mula*

means root and *adhara* means support). The Eucharist is the
body and blood of that love life made human. We nourish
ourselves bodily with that love. It comes to us through wounds,
through vulnerability (*vulnera* in Latin are wounds).
Confirmation is anointing. The Holy Spirit is the Chrism, is the
oil that sinks into our skin and strengthens the muscles, the
sinews. The Church is the body of Christ (socially) as we are the
body of Christ corporally. Our relations with each other are as
resurrected beings, as Gods. We connect as 'persons' who
transcend their 'nature'. Persons can rise from the dead, can
relate to the Trinity, can reach each other without recourse to
physical tactility. *Noli me tangere* refers to the 'me' that has
gone beyond located corporality, that has risen from the dead,
but who is still 'me' as I always was and always will be now and
forever. We are the body of Christ raised from the dead. Our
communion as persons is the visible face of Christ as this has
become distributed through the universe in the Spirit. We are
icons of that cosmic presence, symbols of the world as the
world should be. The final tarot is the trump card, the triumph
of the resurrection. The world is to be understood neither as an
organism nor as a mechanism, it is a work of art; it is
movement and it is rhythm. And if we are pure of heart we can
syncopate our basic rhythm to the divine rhythm and be taken
up into the dance of eternity. Creativity and joy are at the root of
creation, as it was in the beginning, is now, and ever shall be,
world without end.

PART III

TAROT, TITANIC AND THE TWIN TOWERS

In March and April 2002 I held a seminar on the tarot cards at Glenstal Abbey called 'Tuesdays with the Tarot'. I began by using them to meditate upon the events of the previous September when the twin towers of the New York World Trade Centre were destroyed by suicide pilots who had hijacked ordinary commercial planes for this purpose. So many reactions to this ruthless invasion had been heard since that date, the planet was awash with verbiage. This was an occasion to use the tarot cards to help a more mature, less myopic reflection on these events, which seemed to mark the beginning of the twenty-first century in a way somewhat akin to the sinking of the Titanic at the beginning of the twentieth. There was a symbolic dimension to both events, which might be gleaned from a wider horizon and a reading of the signs of the times.

I selected five cards with my group: The Tower was the first. We placed it in the centre. Many who had never seen the cards before were amazed at the pertinence of this picture: two people falling from a tower that is on fire. It had been struck at the top by lightning. Around this centre we placed the cards corresponding to the date of the tragedy: card 9 was the Hermit, placed to the left of the tower; card 11 was Strength, placed to the right; card 1 for the year was the Magician; and the Zero before the one gave us the Fool. These we placed below and above the central card respectively. This cross is one way of spreading the cards. The positions taken up by each card are supposed to read clockwise from the top as they surround the card in the centre:

1 = This is what it is about.
2 = This path may be exciting, but it should be avoided.
3 = This path is the right one.
4 = This is where it leads.

Our method was to concentrate on these cards for a week and then to record the various synchronicities that happened during that week, garnering from each of these whatever might be relevant to our discussions the following Tuesday. Accompanying these sessions was an exhibition of paintings on the Tarot cards[1] by the Dublin artist Lorcan Walshe. These were first exhibited in 1987.

I became interested in the Tarot, the artist noted, through the writings of Carl Jung. The Tarot, Jung surmised, were intrinsically a map of the subconscious. In the Major Arcana, Jung believed, is the archetypal journey through life: each card describing a particular aspect of the psyche. I saw the Major Arcana as a symbolic structure that would enable me to portray the human condition in an autobiographical manner. I decided to paint the Major Arcana on a miniature scale in accordance with the tradition of transmitting powerful visual images from a limited surface area. I used imagery from the history of art and from the twentieth century in combination with established symbolism of the Major Arcana. I included portraits of acquaintances who embodied the particular archetype a card represented. Occasionally all traditional imagery has been abandoned and replaced with relevant modern symbolism.[2]

The example he gives here is precisely the Tower (cf the last plate in the colour section of this book[3]): 'The figure in the foreground is from my "Artist and the Bomb", one of my nuclear war paintings of 1986. In the background is the Hiroshima Dome.' Why should this artist in 1987 have chosen this symbol to represent the Tower card of the major arcana of the tarot? In 1945 the first atom bomb was dropped on the Japanese city of Hiroshima by a single US aircraft, as a result of a joint decision by President Truman of the United States and Prime Minister Attlee of Great Britain. The bomb killed 75,000 to 80,000 people, and many others were severely burned or later suffered from radiation sickness, while the city was almost completely destroyed.

The first thing I need to clarify is that the vast majority of Irish people, including myself (my mother was American), were and are in complete sympathy with the United States of America in their horror and loss. Although there are a number of vociferous and high profile Irish journalists who are anti-American for various reasons, they are a minority. The rest of us support and admire our most successful and generous ally and friend, as the following account illustrates. On Friday, 14 September 2001, there was a National Day of Mourning in Ireland and the nation essentially shut down. Churches throughout the country were filled to overflowing as people took time to remember the dead, injured and bereaved, and to show solidarity with the people of the United States. President Mary McAleese spoke for the vast majority of us:

> On this National Day of Mourning we take time to reflect on the horrendous events of the past few days in the United States. These horrible scenes represent an attack on the very foundations of our human dignity. We are sad, shocked, sickened, grieving, disbelieving, outraged, frightened all at once. We are only beginning to hear the human stories, the unbearable reports of final phone calls of love, of the heroism of so many, the loss of so many. These stories will continue to unfold for many days and weeks to come, bringing with them a growing realisation of the full extent of the pain and sorrow that is the gruesome legacy of these awful acts of hatred. The people of the United States hold a special place in the hearts of all of us here in Ireland. The roots go down through the centuries and are as strong today as they ever were. Our first thoughts therefore are with the American people as they try to cope with the magnitude of what has happened in their great country. To the bereaved, the injured and to those awaiting news of their loved ones, we send our prayers, our deepest sympathy and our support.

She ended her address:

> This National Day of Mourning is a very special opportunity for all of us to show solidarity with our brothers and sisters in the United States of America. It sends a message across the Atlantic and indeed around the globe that Ireland too is broken-hearted and grieving at the unconscionable waste of life we have witnessed this week. God bless those in the

United States, those in Ireland and all those men, women and little children throughout the world who have been personally, profoundly affected by this tragedy. May God guide us safely through these troubled days.

There is no doubt that the deed which was done was horrific and unconscionable. Nobody denies the extent of the tragedy; nobody suggests that this was not a most dastardly deed. In this situation we, especially in Ireland, were all Americans. This attack was against the Western World. The community attacked and destroyed in and around the World Trade Centre was an international community. This was the hub of Western economy. We are all together in this; we feel a sympathy with America which borders on identification. But the question is: how do we respond to such horror? And there is all the difference in the world between sympathising with America under attack and sympathising with the reaction of America to that attack.

The sinking of the Titanic was a symptomatic disaster of the twentieth century, as were the Twin Towers for the twenty-first. These were signs of the times and should be read from a deeper level beneath themselves and within ourselves. Why was this calamity symptomatic of the century we have just entered?

As the seminar began I received a copy of the Winter 2002 edition of *The American Scholar*, which was devoted to 9/11/01.[4] In an article called 'The Skyscraper and the Airplane', Adam Goodheart points out that these two constructions were born side by side in the American Midwest. The Wright brothers in Ohio were responsible for the first powered aircraft. By 1907 they were able to remain airborne for 45 minutes. In 1927 Charles Lindberg successfully completed the first transatlantic flight. Meanwhile, the skyscraper was born out of the commercial need for space in cities where land was scarce and rents were high. The word 'skyscraper' hadn't been associated with buildings before these became part of the Chicago landscape. The word was coined in England in the 1780s to describe the Duke of Bedford's exceptionally large racehorse, which won the Epsom Derby in 1789. By 1932 The Empire State Building in New York was the tallest building in the world and remained such until the 1970s. From 1970 to 1974 the World

Trade Centre, at 412 metres (1,350 ft), was the tallest until the Sears Tower in Chicago beat it by 5 metres (104 ft). These buildings could not have happened unless the century that produced them also invented cheap, high-quality structural steel, which Goodheart describes as the first revolutionary architectural invention since the Romans created the arch and the dome two millenia before. This turned buildings into vertebrates rather than crustaceans: they could stand slender and tall without huge carapaces of supporting masonry. The other less flamboyant but equally necessary inventions were high-speed lifts, electric lighting, central heating, fire escapes, telephones and flush toilets. The felling of the Twin Towers as we witnessed it could not have happened on 9/11/1901. These 176,000 tons of fabricated structural steel was a landmark in welding history in the last quarter of the twentieth century. A Boeing 707, the largest plane flying when the building was planned, was catered for in the design and would have been absorbable. The excursion monitor on the roof of the towers did not even register the 1993 bombing. The world had to wait for the invention of the Boeing 767. According to Stanford University Professor Steven Block,[5] the energy generated by a fuel-laden Boeing 757 or 767 colliding into a World Trade Centre tower is roughly equivalent to one-twentieth of the energy of the atomic bomb dropped on Hiroshima, Japan on 6 August 1945. Ignited fuel generated 90 per cent of the energy in the explosion. A Boeing 767's fuel capacity is roughly 23,980 gallons, and a Boeing 757 carries roughly 11,466 gallons of fuel. It is likely that the terrorists had intentionally taken over planes scheduled to travel across the country because they'd be carrying more fuel and would therefore cause more devastating explosions upon impact.

As in the case of the Titanic, a sinister mate had been prepared alongside. The 767 twin-engined jumbo jet had been put into service only nineteen years before September 11, 2001. 'Strut and brace, spar and rib formed the bones of the plane as they did of the skyscraper, and the airplane, too, would become a sort of capsule of human amenities ... a mobile life-support system.'[6] Both these structures had to have been brought to the particular pitch of refinement that allowed one of them to become the deadly weapon of destruction of the other. Neither could have achieved the kind of insertion and implosion that caused such total disintegration before this twenty-first century, which has presented us with such incredible advances in every level of science and technology. Goodheart reminds us of Tolstoy's character Levin in *Anna Karenina*, who is terrified by the birth of his first child, 'for he realises that he has brought into the world a new means for him to be hurt beyond all previous imagining.'7

One of the ironies of architecture is that Minoru Yamasaki, who designed the World Trade Centre, was, according to Goodheart, afraid of heights. He once wrote that in a world of perfect freedom he would have created nothing but one-storey buildings overlooking fields of flowers.

At the same moment that the planes hit the towers, Maria Burnett-Gaudiani was watching from midtown Manhattan. She phoned her brother Graham Burnett and both their diary records are published in this same journal in an article called 'Double Exposure.'8 For the previous year Maria had been working on an architectural model of the two towers for a senior-year architecture studio at Princeton University. In 1997 her professor had proposed connecting the two towers as a conceptual project. What Maria eventually came up with was an answer to the 'phallarchitects' who had created the Twin Towers. True, her proposal was a structurally unsound and inefficient form for a tall building, but, as she says, 'I loved the shape of the two towers outstretched as if to kiss over the skyline.'9 'Her solution was, in her brother's words, a conceptual work of considerable genius. Instead of creating a bridge of some sort, Maria undertook a much more ambitious reconfiguration of the towers themselves. She began by extending the footprint of each building so that their adjacent edges overlapped. Then she carved out a space between them, leaving the buildings linked at their bases and their crowns. But the drama, formal elegance, and critical intelligence of the design lay in the way she treated the negative space she had created between the towers. By cutting away their edges in a sensuous curve, she deftly conjured a new "gateway to Manhattan", a gore-shaped aperture more than 90 storeys high, faced with glass, a slit in the skyline.'10 Maria and her studio mates had taken to calling her design the World Trade Yoni, this being the Hindu symbol of the vulva representing the feminine principle.

Returning to Adam Goodheart, he points out that if the skyscraper's crude phallic thrust is male, like a massive two-finger sign towards the Atlantic, the airplane embodies the female principle: 'Entering, we pass into a place that promises – if rarely quite delivering – all the amenities of the womb: shelter, nourishment, warmth, dimness, sleep.'[11]

September 11 was a nightmare. It breached that frontier between the world of waking and the world of sleep, between the conscious and the unconscious. As Goodheart says, 'like all true nightmares, it was grafted together out of pre-existing elements, fragments of our waking lives and our imaginations'. We had in fact seen it happen before in movies, 'and when the towers did fall, we watched with the horror of witnesses to a death half foreseen, in dreams and shadowy portents'.[12]

This is why artists and the arcanum of the tarot can help us to situate the reality of what happened. If we place the tragedy against the background of the five cards, the Tower, the Fool, the Magician, the Hermit and Strength, we are able to provide an unconscious safety net which prevents us from falling too deeply into the fissure in the foundation that the event can tempt us to probe. There are five men and one woman in this selection. The three men are aware of the feminine principle within themselves and at least two of them are in touch with the unconscious world. The card with the woman opening the lion's mouth is warning us about the too easy solution.

But let's begin in the middle with the Tower. Dramatic liberation, breakthrough to greater freedom, breakdown of a false self-image. 'An inflated consciousness,' Jung tells us, 'is hypnotised by itself and can therefore not be argued with. It inevitably dooms itself to calamities that must strike it dead.'[13] These are accepted readings of the meaning of this card. The gates to the underworld have been breached. The task is to liberate the prisoner within who has been sold into bondage. 'Something there is that doesn't love a wall.' Surrounded by walls, we cannot see beyond them. This card symbolises the destruction of those walls. 'A collapse of the conscious attitude is no small matter; it always feels like the end of the world, as though everything had tumbled back into original chaos. One feels delivered up, disoriented, like a rudderless ship that is abandoned to the moods of the elements. So at least it seems. In reality, however, one has fallen back upon the collective unconscious, which now takes over the leadership.'[14] What did these twin towers symbolise? To those around, and that means all of us who gloried in this spectacular human landscape, it spoke of the eventual victory of capitalism at the end of the twentieth century. Hubris, pride? Economic wealth, gained at the expense of poorer nations? National pride? All of these are possible interpretations from the other side of the tracks. For instance, here is Kate Connolly reporting for *The Guardian* in Berlin the month after the 9/11 attack:

A leading German fashion designer said yesterday there should be no regrets about the destruction of the World Trade Centre because it symbolised capitalism at its worst. 'I don't regret that the twin towers are no longer standing because they symbolised capitalist arrogance,' Wolfgang Joop, 56, told the Austrian magazine *Profil*. When questioned by the tabloid *Bild*, he qualified his comments by adding: 'September 11 set a learning process in motion because the twin towers, as symbols of capitalist arrogance, have fallen.' Joop added that he nevertheless opposed 'violence, murder and terror'. The designer criticised the chancellor, Gerhard Schröder, for expressing Germany's 'unlimited solidarity' with the US after the attacks. He said Mr Schröder's behaviour reminded him of the Nazi era. 'Schröder's pushing himself into the limelight and wants to show he's running with the rest,' he said. 'But we Germans are wary of those who run with the rest because we've had terrible experiences with this. Such behaviour reminds me of the Nazi era.'[15]

Apart from perceptions of the towers from a distance and from the outside, there must have been some misgivings about the kind of lifestyle imposed upon those living inside these buildings. People living inside such towers must have lived an 'unnatural' existence. Imagine life inside those layers of glass boxes. Some must have been moving from an underground garage in their own skyscraper apartment, through city traffic in another mobile bowl, to their place of work: yet another underground car park leading to a glass box in the sky. Can a life be lived so many storeys above the earth, from which it has been irretrievably cemented off? Is this a natural existence or is it a glass menagerie, a multi-storeyed goldfish bowl, from which the world must eventually be grateful to have been released?

At the base of the tarot tower where the two falling figures are about to land, there are two white stones with writing on them. In the book of Revelation 3:17 'anyone who has ears to hear with' is asked to listen to what the Spirit is saying; and to those who are victorious in this way: 'I will give a white stone with a new name written on it, known only to the one who receives it.' The search for such a white stone for America in the twenty-first century is surely the most pressing investigation of ground zero territory.

Above and below the card of the Tower are the two cards that spell out the year of the disaster. Ground Zero they called the bombed-out tower site as if referring to the card above the Tower. 'As above, so below,' is the axiom of the major arcana of the tarot. The Fool leads us towards a new humility, one blasted deep into the underground. The wisdom gained from both the Magician and the Fool must surely inform whatever architecture is devised to replace the one that for so long dominated the skyline of our Western world. Ground Zero: we have, as a world, been here before. The twentieth century was lived for the most part at this nadir. James Conrad wrote *Heart of Darkness*, published in 1902, when he discovered what humanity was really like. In a letter of 1895 he writes: 'All my work is produced unconsciously (so to speak) and ... it isn't in me to improve what has got itself written.' This kind of art is inspired by ground zero, the ultimate edge of the human condition. It comes from a depth where its authorship is no longer quite traceable. T. S. Eliot read Conrad's book and wrote *The Wasteland*, from a corresponding ground zero in his own beleaguered unconscious in 1922, between two world wars:

What are the roots that clutch, what branches grow
Out of this stony rubbish? Son of man,
You cannot say, or guess, for you know only
A heap of broken images, where the sun beats,
And the dead tree gives no shelter, the cricket no relief,
And the dry stone no sound of water. Only

There is shadow under this red rock,
(Come in under the shadow of this red rock),
And I will show you something different from either
Your shadow at morning striding behind you
Or your shadow at evening rising to meet you;
I will show you fear in a handful of dust.

Card number one, as in the first year of a new century,
represents cleverness, skill, self-confidence, the capacity to
create your own life, your own destiny. Such fluency is based
upon harmonious interchange and balanced equilibrium
between consciousness and the unconscious. Those who have
learned the wisdom that the tarot can teach are more likely to be
able to show us the way forward. The card of the Magician also
forces us to think the unthinkable, formulated by at least one
European artist: the felling of the Twin Towers was in some
way a work of art. In the week after the September 11 onslaught,
the German avant-garde composer Karlheinz Stockhausen, 73,
was forced to apologise after describing the terrorists' actions
as 'the greatest work of art one can imagine'. Four of his
concerts were cancelled in the furore after his remarks. If one
looked at the picture on the front page of every newspaper in
the world the day after the 9/11 happenings, and if you did not
know what was being represented, you might have been
forgiven for imagining that these were photographs of abstract
paintings of the most exquisite beauty. The lines and
colourings of the stately buildings surrounded by blue skies
and with a pink turning towards mauve circle at their centre
could have been a contemporary artwork.[16] I am sure that this
is not what Stockhausen had in mind, nor do I pretend to have
an interpretation of his enigmatic statement, later apologised
for and maybe withdrawn. But it is there as an utterance which
forces us to think. And what it forces me to think is this: if art is
a way of shocking the world into seeing and understanding
something it had not seen before and was unlikely ever to see,
then this event might qualify for this description.

Osama bin Laden has become another byword for the
devil in our Western world. His name has joined Beelzebub
and Mephistopheles as incarnating the personal principle of
evil. As such he can perform that most important role of the
devil, he can act as Lucifer, the bearer of light, the one who

forces home truths into unwilling consciousness. The myth of the Egyptian Sun God Ra's journey at sea during the night-time describes, in C. G. Jung's terms, how the totally neglected side of ourselves is raised from the depths and hoisted into daylight. The treasure that is hardest to find of all our myths, legends, fairytales, is our fourth, unconscious function. At the deepest point of his journey, Ra encounters the greatest of all dangers. Apophis, the snake of the night-time sea, sucks dry the underground Nile with one single gulp so Ra's boat gets stuck on a sandbank, ground zero. The Sun God cannot continue the journey and there would be no new morning for our world if it were not for Seth. Seth forces the snake to spit out the water, which allows the boat to continue its journey. And who was Seth who induced the serpent to vomit up the secrets that would help us on our way? He was, of course, the devil, the arch villain, the greatest enemy of the Sun God during the day. But here at midnight, at the point zero of the new millennium, he is the only one who can see to it that the boat moves, and in the right direction. Such a thought was so outrageous to the Egyptians that they dared not pronounce his name. So they whispered: 'The greatest sorcerer of all time helps the great Ra here.' But in truth, everyone knew who the great sorcerer was. And the great truth of this arcana is that in the darkest hour, the ground zero, the black-and-white judgements of daylight consciousness collapse.[17] The one whom we have experienced as our greatest enemy is the one who can help us achieve the breakthrough which we need to make, to become the completion and the perfection of who we are and who we were meant to be. This is the meaning of that most private and most secret of all injunctions: 'Love your enemy as yourself.'

The eleventh card, in the second position to the right of the Tower as we face it, is the option to be avoided. Eleven is the card for Strength or Force. This card can refer either to the reaction after the event, or to the possible replacement of the buildings destroyed. Despite the impression which the Twin Towers may have made on others, the original architect saw these as providing a very positive mystique:

> There are a few very influential architects who sincerely believe that all buildings must be 'strong'. The word 'strong' in this context seems to connote 'powerful' – that is, each

building should be a monument to the virility of our society. These architects look with derision upon attempts to build a friendly, more gentle kind of building... Although it is inevitable for architects who admire [the] great monumental buildings of Europe to strive for the quality most evident in them, grandeur, the elements of mysticism and power, basic to cathedrals and palaces, are also incongruous today, because the buildings we build for our times are for a totally different purpose.

These words could not be more relevant today after the untimely destruction of his twin towers. Even more so his initial hopes for his huge skyscrapers:

I feel this way about it. World trade means world peace and consequently the World Trade Center buildings in New York ... had a bigger purpose than just to provide room for tenants. The World Trade Center is a living symbol of man's dedication to world peace ... beyond the compelling need to make this a monument to world peace, the World Trade Center should, because of its importance, become a representation of man's belief in humanity, his need for individual dignity, his beliefs in the cooperation of men, and through cooperation, his ability to find greatness.[18]

How could it have ended up being quite the opposite: an enemy target, as the embodiment of world-dominating capitalism. Lorcan Walshe, through the sixteenth arcana of the tarot tower, refers us back to Hiroshima 56 years before. Is it a question of an ego for an ego, a tower for a tower? Whatever about the motivation, the answer to the murder of 3,000 people is surely not to kill another 3,000.

To the hawks, as opposed to the doves, any card marked Strength must read: Adamantine, burly, crushing, drive, energy, force, geopolitics, hammer and tongs, indomitable, impregnable iron, jump-start, knock-out, lambast, muscular might, nuclear war, oblige, power, quench, robust, rock-ribbed, steel, strength, tough, unbridled, violent, war, xenophobia, yoke, zap. Such, indeed were the remarks by President Bush in 'Photo Opportunity with the National Security Team' in the Cabinet Room on September 12, 2001:

The deliberate and deadly attacks which were carried out yesterday against our country were more than acts of terror. They were acts of war. This will require our country to unite in steadfast determination and resolve. Freedom and democracy are under attack. The American people need to know that we're facing a different enemy than we have ever faced. This enemy hides in shadows, and has no regard for human life. This is an enemy who preys on innocent and unsuspecting people, then runs for cover. But it won't be able to run for cover forever. This is an enemy that tries to hide. But it won't be able to hide forever. This is an enemy that thinks its harbours are safe. But they won't be safe forever. This enemy attacked not just our people, but all freedom-loving people everywhere in the world. The United States of America will use all our resources to conquer this enemy. We will rally the world. We will be patient, we will be focused, and we will be steadfast in our determination. This battle will take time and resolve. But make no mistake about it: we will win... This will be a monumental struggle of good versus evil. But good will prevail.

War is the image used to describe what happened. Such imagery may be misleading. This could not be war in any recognisable sense. And, after 1945, war is no longer a viable option on this planet. A more appropriate image might be used: the image of disease. Terrorism is not an identifiable enemy; it is a universal plague. It requires methods different from and more comprehensive than warfare. We have to change tactics and try to unite the world in an emergency offensive against terrorism. Part of this effort will be to remove the perception of the United States as bully boy and warlord. Ulrich Wickert, a German television presenter, caused an outcry shortly after 9/11 by saying in a live broadcast that the behaviour of George Bush and Osama bin Laden was 'comparable'. But such perceptions are not confined to commentators outside America. Ramsey Clark, former US attorney general was reported in *The Sun Magazine* in an interview with Derrick Jensen, published in August 2001, a month before the September 11 disaster, saying about US foreign policy:

Our overriding purpose, from the beginning right through
to the present day, has been world domination ... that is to
build and maintain the capacity to coerce everybody else on
the planet: non-violently, if possible, and violently, if
necessary. But the purpose of foreign policy of domination
is not just to make the rest of the world jump through
hoops; the purpose is to facilitate our exploitation of
resources.

Whether this view be true or false, it represents a growing
perception around the world and one which needs to be worked
upon at many levels to remove any pertinence it may have had
in the past. 'Strength' does not mean domination; nor does it
mean 'weakness'. There is a way of being firm without being
fascist; of removing danger without annihilation; of defending
without demolishing. Whatever the response to the destruction
and the proposal for replacement of the World Trade Centre,
the eleventh major arcana of the tarot requires that these be
infused by the feminine principle.

    The ninth card, situated where it is, shows us the
outcome of our taking the right direction: it is about becoming
conscious of who one really is: learning one's true name. Why
would anyone want to take out the World Trade Centre? We
must surely spend some time wandering through the rubble
with our tiny lantern deciphering the clues that might lead us
towards some answers to that question. The hermit is an artist.
This card is what such art is all about.

    In his 1970 Nobel lecture, Alexander Solzhenitsyn
(1918–) made a distinction between two kinds of artist: 'One
artist sees himself as the creator of an independent spiritual
world: he hoists onto his shoulders the task of creating this
world, of peopling it and of bearing the all-embracing
responsibility for it... Another artist, recognising a higher
power above, gladly works as a humble apprentice beneath
God's heaven.' The three circumstances which reduced
Solzhenitsyn to 'ground zero' in his own life and which forced
him to find what he called The First Circle, were those three
curses of the twentieth century: war, cancer and the
concentration camps. The quest of this quintessentially
twentieth-century man and Russian artist is to lay bare for the
rest of us the seat of the heart, the point zero of human

experience, upon which he himself stumbled through a series of, humanly speaking, unfortunate accidents, but from which disasters he gained access to the richest dimension of human existence. In *The Gulag Archipelago*, Solzhenitsyn, gifted with a memory of almost total recall, shows how communism unwittingly bestowed on twentieth-century humanity, in the persons of those dissidents who refused to conform to its image of itself, the inestimable richness of true self-awareness. In *Cancer Ward* the preoccupation is the same. 'The infernal circle of cancer' forces the patient to the same interior vanishing point. For Solzhenitsyn, cancer is the disease that symbolises twentieth-century Western society. As an indiscriminate multiplication of cells in parts of the human organism, it mirrors the proliferation of prison cells and concentration camps throughout the diseased body politic of Europe. As a personal illness it can lead the individual patient to that same inner sanctuary which he describes in *The First Circle*. This point zero of human existence he calls the circle of innermost interiority. The action of the novel with the same name takes place in the special prison of Mavrino. The movement is a descent into hell. "No, my dear Sir," one prisoner is told, "you are in hell, just as before. But you have graduated to its best and highest circle – the first circle."[19] Mavrino is a former manor house converted into a prison. The focal point of this place 'had once been the sanctuary of the chapel in this former country house, but now had also been converted into a cell. The door was always shut and it was covered from top to bottom with sheet iron. It was known as the "heavenly gates". The altar had been removed and the new purpose of the space was an acoustics laboratory where 'the objective was to find a way of identifying voices ... and to discover what it is that makes every human voice unique.'"[20] The inner sanctuary of the human prison, ground zero, the first circle at the seat of the human heart, is the acoustics laboratory where the prisoner can identify another voice, while at the same time discovering the uniqueness of one's own.

The Irish poet and Nobel Laureate, Seamus Heaney, wrote a poem specifically about the September 11 disaster, 'which tried to stand firm against the chaos of the event'. He confessed that he felt called to do something and his response had been a translation of one of Horace's *Odes*, written in the first century BCE:

Horace and the Thunder[21]

After Horace, Odes, 1, 34

Anything can happen. You know how Jupiter
Will mostly wait for clouds to gather head
Before he hurls the lightning? Well, just now,
He galloped his thunder-cart and his horses

Across a clear blue sky. It shook the earth
And the clogged underneath, the River Styx,
The winding streams, the Atlantic shore itself.
Anything can happen, the tallest things

Be overturned, those in high places daunted,
Those overlooked esteemed. Stropped-beak Fortune
Swoops, making the air gasp, tearing off
Crests for sport, letting them drop wherever.

Ground gives. The heavens' weight
Lifts up off Atlas like a kettle lid,
Capstones shift, nothing resettles right.
Telluric ash and fire-spores boil away.

This translation suggests that there is nothing new under the
sun. Even though the tragedy of the Twin Towers seems to us
to be incomparable and unprecedented, it is one link in a chain
of previous and connected happenings. The poem, he said at a
lecture he gave at the Royal College of Surgeons of Ireland in
Dublin, was equal to a need people felt in the wake of the
terrorist attacks – a need for words that would be equal to
peoples' shock and bewilderment at having to live in a newly
dangerous world. When circumstances are at their most
bewildering and overwhelming, people often want 'an
articulation' that will act as 'a momentary stay against
confusion'. The good of poetry, he argued, is in finding words
that allow the inner world of language and feelings to connect
with the outer world of facts and happenings. 'Words that stay
firm when we press upon them, words that won't let us down
when we ask them to take the strain of reality.'[22] 'Anything can
happen', both Horace and Heaney are agreed. Jupiter, highest

judge over Gods and human beings, can ride a chariot wherever he will. The lightning flash was one of Jupiter's attributes. By Jove, as common parlance remembers his other name. Asklepios was slain by Zeus' thunderbolt. Lightning has always been experienced by human beings as a manifestation of divine energy. Such a god figures in Buddhism as a symbol of the light of truth, which hypocrisy or falsehood cannot withstand. Human consciousness is in the presence of those primary forces which constitute its basic reality. Whoever comes near to these realities is near the fire. But in this instance the earth is shaken and the clogged underneath, the Styx, has somehow been unclogged. It is an ill wind galloping across a clear blue sky that blows no good, that fails to make some air gasp. We should not rebuild too quickly until we have examined the ground zero opened and exposed. This event blew all of us into the realms of the unconscious, into the territory of the tarot cards. As Seamus Heaney put it: 'There was a feeling that a crack had run through the foundations ... that the border between the imaginable and the possible had been eradicated. For many, and Americans in particular, danger and terror crossed from the realm of fantasy into a historical record. A catastrophe happened in full view of the nations of the earth. Neither the common mind nor the common language was prepared for it.'[23] The suggestion being made in this book is that at the beginning of the twenty-first century, the event of the Twin Towers has, in fact, stopped us in our tracks and forced us to learn another language, one which is hidden in deeper layers of the unconscious and for which the major arcana of the tarot can act as a beginner's alphabet.

NOTES

NOTES

PART I

CHAPTER ONE

1. Virgil, *The Aeneid*, II, l. 49.
2. Alexander Pope, *Moral Essays*, line 149.
3. Iris Murdoch, 'The Fire and the Sun', in *Existentialists and Mystics*, ed. Peter Conradi (Chatto & Windus, London, 1997), p. 403. (Hereafter referred to as EM with page number in the text itself.) In what follows about the Greeks I am indebted to Iris Murdoch both for the understanding, which is similar to my own, but, more importantly, for the felicitous expression of this understanding, which was her incomparable gift both as philosopher and as artist.
4. F.M. Cornford, *Plato's Cosmology* (Kegan Paul, London, 1937).
5. Plotinus, *Enneads*, III, 6.6.
6. This would correspond to the Hebrew word *Hatta* and the Greek word *Hamartia*, which translate our word 'sin' and which mean 'missing the mark', not achieving our full potential.
7. I have approached the unconscious in terms of art in three previous books: *Kissing the Dark* (Veritas, Dublin, 1999); *The Haunted Inkwell* (Columba, Dublin, 2001); and *Anchoring the Altar* (Veritas, Dublin, 2002).

CHAPTER TWO

1. A set of these cards was given to me by Liz Shannon in 1991 when I was staying with her in Boston.
2. Ronald Decker, Thierry Depaulis, and Michael Dummett, *A Wicked Pack of Cards: The Origins of Tarot Occultism* (Duckworth, London, 1996); Ronald Decker and Michael Dummett, *A History of the Occult Tarot 1870–1970* (Duckworth, London, 2002). A review of these books was first brought to my attention by William Fennelly.
3. *A History of the Occult Tarot*, op. cit. p. 177.

4. Morgan Robertson, *The Wreck of the Titan Or, Futility &
Morgan Robertson The Man* (Amereon Ltd, New York, 1995).
This is a reprint of the 1912 version of the same book, originally
printed as a story in 1898. The existence of this work was
brought to my attention in 1992 by Ferenc Szücs.
5. Ibid., p. 2.
6. Ibid. p. 22.
7. Michael Talbot, *The Holographic Universe* (Harper, New
York, 1992), p. 212. This book was sent to me by Maria Janis
Cooper.

CHAPTER THREE

1. The title of this chapter is the one used by Kathleen Raine
in a lecture she gave to the Yeats International Summer School
at Sligo on 15 August 1968, later printed and published by
Dolmen Press (Dublin, 1972). A first edition of this lecture was
given to me by Ronnie O'Gorman when I first began writing
this book. The lecture was later included in: Kathleen Raine,
Yeats the Initiate (Dolmen Press, Dublin, 1986).
2. *The Letters of W. B. Yeats*, ed. Alan Wade (1954), p. 211.
3. George Mills Harper, *Yeats's Golden Dawn: The Influence
of the Hermetic Order of the Golden Dawn on the Life and Art
of W. B. Yeats* (Aquarian Press, 1987).
4. Kathleen Raine, *Yeats the Initiate* (Dolmen Press, Dublin,
1986).
5. R. F. Foster: *W. B. Yeats, A Life, vol. 1, The Apprentice Mage*
(Oxford University Press, 1997).
6. W. B. Yeats, *Autobiographies* (Macmillan, London, 1955),
pp. 115–116.
7. Ronald Decker, Thierry Depaulis and Michael Dummett, *A
Wicked Pack of Cards: the Origins of Tarot Occultism* (London,
1996); Ronald Decker & Michael Dummett, *A History of the
Occult Tarot 1870-1970* (Duckworth, London, 2002), p. 92f.
Hereafter this work is referred to in the text as HOC with a page
number.
8. A. Norman Jeffares, *W. B. Yeats: A New Biography* (Arena,
1988), p. 77.
9. George Mills Harper, *Yeats's Golden Dawn*, op. cit.
10. *William Butler Yeats Memoirs*, edited by Denis Donoghue
(1972), p. 27.

11. A. Norman Jeffares, *W. B. Yeats, A New Biography*, op. cit., p. 115.
12. George Mills Harper, *Yeats's Golden Dawn: The Influence of the Hermetic Order of the Golden Dawn on the Life and Art of W. B. Yeats* (Aquarian Press, 1987).
13. Kathleen Raine, *Yeats the Initiate* (1986), pp. 216–220.
14. A. Norman Jeffares, *W. B. Yeats, A New Biography*, op. cit., p. 156.
15. Kathleen Raine, *Yeats the Initiate*, op. cit., p. 212.
16. These texts are reproduced in full in Appendix H and K of George Mills Harper, *Yeats's Golden Dawn*, op. cit., pp. 246–68.
17. Ibid.
18. Ibid.
19. W. B. Yeats, *Explorations* (1962), p. 417.
20. A. Norman Jeffares, *W. B. Yeats, A New Biography*, op. cit., p. 164.
21. W. B. Yeats, 'A final letter to the Adepti of R.R. et A.C. on the Present Crisis', reproduced in its entirety in Appendix H, George Mills Harper, *Yeats's Golden Dawn*, op. cit., p. 248.
22. W. B. Yeats, in George Mills Harper, *Yeats's Golden Dawn*, op. cit., p. 268.
23. Ibid., p. 263.
24. Ibid., p. 267.
25. W. B. Yeats, *Essays and Introductions* (1961), p. 28. (Essay on 'Magic' written in 1901.)
26. W. B. Yeats, *Autobiographies*, op. cit., p. 31.
27. W. B. Yeats, *Essays and Introductions*, op. cit., p. 174.
28. Ibid. p. 178.
29. Evelyn Underhill, *Mysticism* (Methuen, London, 1960), p. 149f.
30. Ibid., pp. 70–72, 151.
31. Yeats, cited in George Mills Harper, *Yeats's Golden Dawn*, op. cit., pp. 58–59.
32. W. B. Yeats, *Essays and Introductions*, op. cit., p. 518.
33. Kathleen Raine, *Yeats the Initiate*, op. cit.
34. Elizabeth Butler Cullingford, *Gender and History in Yeats's Love Poetry* (Cambridge University Press, 1993), p. 111f.
35. Ibid, p. 111.
36. Anne Saddlemeyer, *Becoming George, The Life of Mrs W. B. Yeats* (Oxford University Press, 2002), pp. 119–123.
37. Elizabeth Butler Cullingford, op.cit., p. 248.

38. Ibid., p. 253.

39. Anne Saddlemeyer, op. cit., pp. 119–120.

40. W. B. Yeats, *Explorations*, Selected by Mrs W. B. Yeats (Macmillan, London, 1962), p. 404.

41. Anne Saddlemeyer, op. cit., pp. 121–122.

42. T.S. Eliot, 'The Poetry of W. B. Yeats', *The Southern Review*, vol. VII, no. 3 (Winter, 1942), pp. 442–454.

CHAPTER FOUR

1. John Carey, 'Poetic License', *The Sunday Times*, 9 March 1997, sec. 8, p. 1.

2. William Butler Yeats, *Four Years 1887–1891* (The Cuala Press, Dublin, 1921), pp. 4–5. This first edition was given to me by Joan McBreen. It was later published in W. B. Yeats, *Autobiographies*, op. cit., pp. 115–116.

3. Vincent Foster Hopper, *Medieval Number Symbolism, Its Sources, Meaning, and Influence on Thought and Expression* (Columbia University Press, New York, 1938).

4. Ibid., pp. 114–115.

5. Henry Morley, *Medieval Tales*, (London, 1844), pp. 155–157

6. W. B. Yeats, *Essays and Introductions*, op. cit., pp 400–401.

7. A. N. Whitehead, *Science and the Modern World* 1st edition (Mentor, New York, 1960), p. 57.

8. David Bohm, *Wholeness and the Implicate Order*, Routledge & Kegan Paul, London, Boston, 1980, p. 48.

9. C. G. Jung, *The Structure and Dynamics of the Psyche*, The Collected Works, vol. 8 (Bollingen Series XX, New York, 1960), pp. 509–511.

10. Ibid., pp. 437–438.

11. The words are from the Delphic Oracle and were inscribed by Carl Jung over the door of his house (*Vocatus Atque Non Vocatus, Deus Aderit*).

CHAPTER FIVE

1. C. G.Jung, *Collected Works*, vol. 11 (Bollingen, New York, 1958), pp. 468–469.

2. See my book *Kissing the Dark* (Veritas, Dublin, 1999).

3. *Die Grossen Arcana des Tarot, Meditationen, mit einer*

einführung von Hans Urs Von Balthasar, 2 vols (Herder, Basel, 3rd edition, 1993). The introduction is from pp. ix to xvi. The translation used here is one which Henry O'Shea and I wrote out for the Sophia Conference at Glenstal Abbey in 1996. I came across this book thanks to Treasa O'Driscoll and Diarmuid Rooney. Diarmuid and I later studied it together for two years.

4. *Meditations on the Tarot, A Journey into Christian Hermeticism* (Element Books, Boston, 1991). This translation by Robert A. Powell from the original French manuscript is published in accordance with the author's intentions: anonymously and posthumously.

5. Sallie Nichols, *Jung and Tarot, An Archetypal Journey* (Samuel Weiser, Maine, 1980).

6. Alfred Douglas, *The Tarot* (Arkana, 1991) has useful comments on the numbers for each card, some of which I have used.

PART II – THE MAJOR ARCANA

III   THE EMPRESS

1. Sallie Nichols, *Jung and the Tarot, An Archetypal Journey*, op. cit., p. 103. (Hereafter referred to in the text as SN.)

XI   STRENGTH / FORCE

1. Dylan Thomas, *Collected Poems, 1934–1952* (J.M. Dent, London, 1952), p. 9.

2. W. B. Yeats, *Essays and Introductions*, op. cit., p. 341.

3. John, 10:10; 11:25–26.

XII   THE HANGED MAN

1. Mercia Eliade, *The Forge and the Crucible* (Harper and Row, New York, 1962), p. 117. Quoted in Sallie Nichols, op. cit., p. 219.

2. C. G. Jung, *Psychology and Alchemy*, Complete Works, vol. 12, para. 32. Quoted in Sallie Nichols, op. cit., pp. 222–223.

XIII   DEATH

1. St John of the Cross, Commentary on Stanza 39 of 'The Spiritual Canticle', nos 3 and 4, in *The Collected Works of St John of the Cross*, translated by Kieran Kavanaugh (1999), pp. 622–623.

XV   THE DEVIL

1. Cf. Sallie Nichols, op. cit., p. 266.
2. C. G. Jung, Complete Works, vol. 13, para. 335.
3. C. G. Jung, Complete Works, vol. 10, para. 572; vol. 7, para. 40.

XVII   THE STAR

1. W. B. Yeats, from his poem 'Among School Children' included appropriately in his 1928 collection called *The Tower*.
2. From 'Sailing to Byzantium', from *The Tower* (1928).

XVIII   THE MOON

1. C. G. Jung, The Psychology of Transference' in *The Practice of Psychotherapy*, CW, vol. 16, para. 502.
2. Thomas Mann, *Joseph the Provider, Joseph and his Brothers*, vol. IV (Sphere Books, London, 1968), p. 202.
3. Hajo Banzhaf, *Tarot and the Journey* (Samuel Weiser, Maine, 2000), pp. 192–193.

XVIIII   THE SUN

1. C. G. Jung, *Memories, Dreams, Reflections* (Flamingo Paperback, London, 1983), pp. 221–2.
2. Teilhard de Chardin, *The Future of Man*, (Fount Paperback, 1982), pp 146-156.

XXI   THE WORLD

1. 'The nudity, poverty and humility of Christ.'

2.   Kenneth Clark, *The Naked and the Nude* (Pelican Paperback, London, 1960), p. 22.

3.   Marie-Louise von Franz, *C. G. Jung, His Myth in our Time* (New York, C. G. Jung Foundation, 1975), p. 74. Quoted in Sallie Nichols, op. cit., p. 352.

PART III

TAROT, TITANIC AND THE TWIN TOWERS

1.   These 22 paintings were on loan for the duration of the seminar from Risteárd Mulcahy.

2.   From notes given by the artist to the owner of the paintings at the time of their first exhibition in 1987.

3.   'The Tower' by Lorcan Walshe from his 1987 series on the Major Arcana of the Tarot, with the kind permission of Risteárd Mulcahy and Lorcan Walshe.

4.   *The American Scholar*, published by the Phi Beta Kappa Society, vol. 71, no. 1 (Winter 2002). This magazine is sent to me every year by Rita McConn-Stern.

5.   Block is a professor of applied physics and biological sciences and an expert on national security and terrorism. He spoke at a press conference on the afternoon of September 11, as reported by Jennifer Deitz Berry in *Palo Alto Weekly*, Online Edition, 4 p.m., 11 September 2001.

6.   Adam Goodheart, 'The Skyscraper and the Airplane', *The American Scholar*, op. cit., p. 17.

7.   Ibid., p. 19.

8.   *The American Scholar*, op. cit., pp. 29–37.

9.   Ibid., p. 35.

10. Ibid., p. 30.

11. Ibid., p. 18.

12. Adam Goodheart, *The American Scholar*, op. cit., pp. 13, 19.

13. C. G. Jung, *Complete Works*, op. cit., vol. 12, para. 563.

14. C. G. Jung, *Complete Works*, op. cit., vol. 7, para. 254.

15. *The Guardian*, Tuesday, 16 October 2001.

16. This aspect of the newspaper reportage was pointed out to me by Jo O'Donovan, artist and nun.

17. Hajo Banzhaf, *Tarot and the Journey*, op. cit. pp. 181–183.

18. Minoru Yamasaki quoted in Paul Heyer, *Architects on Architecture: New Directions in America* (Van Nostrand Reinhold, 1993), p. 186.

19. Alexander Solzhenitsyn, *The First Circle* (Collins/Fontana Paperback, 1971), p. 19.

20. Ibid., pp. 25–26, 33.

21. The poem as printed in *The Irish Times*, 19 November 2001.

22. This report of 'The Whole Thing: On the Good of Poetry', which was the annual lecture of the department of international health and tropical medicine delivered by Seamus Heaney, was given by Eithne Donnellan in *The Irish Times*, 6 November 2001.

23. Seamus Heaney, 'The Whole Thing: On the Good of Poetry', as quoted in *The Irish Times*, 6 November 2001.